Transforming the Field

Transforming the Field

Critical Antiracist and Anti-oppressive Perspectives for the Human Services Practicum

Narda Razack

Fernwood Publishing • Halifax

Editing: Eileen Young
Cover photo: Barbara Swanson
Cover design: Larissa Holman
Design and production: Beverley Rach
Printed and bound in Canada by: Hignell Printing Limited

A publication of:
Fernwood Publishing
Box 9409, Station A
Halifax, Nova Scotia
B3K 5S3

Fernwood Publishing Company Limited gratefully acknowledges the financial support of the Department of Canadian Heritage, the Nova Scotia Department of Tourism and Culture and the Canada Council for the Arts for our publishing program.

Le Conseil des Arts | The Canada Council
du Canada | for the Arts

NOVA SCOTIA
Tourism and Culture

National Library of Canada Cataloguing in Publication Data

Razack, Narda
Transforming the field: antiracist and anti-oppressive perspectives for the human services practicum

Includes bibliographical references.
ISBN 1-55266-075-3

1. Social service—Field work—Study and teaching. 2. Minorities in social work education. 3. Social service and race relations. I. Title.

HV11.R39 2002   361.3'2'0711   C2001-904021-0

Contents

Chapter Four

The Agency Context 68

Chapter Five

**Power Dynamics, Knowledge Production and
Social Location: The Role of the Field Instructor** 77

Chapter Six

**The Integrative Seminar as a Pedagogical Tool for
Anti-oppressive Social Work Field Education** 88

Acknowledgements

This book signifies my beginning work as an academic. I came to the university convinced that the community and university should be linked to produce not only skilled social work practitioners but individuals who would invest in the spirit of transformation for social justice and equity. I am thankful for the opportunities to conceptualize what the work in the field truly means and vision how field education can be integrated into the curriculum to shift the boundaries of teaching and practice. I thank the many field instructors who are a source of inspiration as they make theory and practice come alive to the students. I thank the many students who also inspire me with their passion for the profession and practice.

My academic career has been significantly boosted by the friendship, unconditional support and collegiality of Pat Evans. She is a constant reminder that indeed there are just people in this world. Amy Rossiter continues to teach me to take risks and is a friend and colleague of the highest esteem. My friend and true ally in social work, Akua Benjamin, is my rock and helps me to face struggles as they emerge so often in academia. Marty Laurence I thank for constantly teaching me how to negotiate the academic terrain. To my colleagues Rashmi Luther, Bessa Whitmore, Carl James, Ben Carniol and Donna Jeffery, an excellent research assistant, a special thanks for being there for me. I thank Gayla Rogers, Joan Leeson and all the field education coordinators across the country who help to shape some of the words in the text. A special thanks to Sherene Razack who always responds with challenging words and kindness.

I want to also recognize my international partners at the University of The West Indies. My appreciation to Lesley Cooper who came into my life recently and will guide me through the next phase of my work. I am particularly grateful to the staff at Fernwood, particularly Errol Sharpe who accepted the idea, Eileen Young, Brenda Conroy, Larissa Holman and Beverley Rach. My love and gratitude to my sisters, brothers, nephews and nieces in Trinidad and in Canada who always believe in me, cook for me and love me. I thank my mother whose unconditional love sustains me.

Thanks also to my son Emir, who is my constant teacher and a truly good person, and my daughters Sabrina and Yasmin, who are rare treasures and unfailingly supportive. This book is dedicated to Zaim, my partner and friend who continues to amaze me with his inner strengths and goodness and his ability to exude fun and laughter at all times.

Introduction

This text focuses on field education in social work: the primary objective is to create critical discourse about issues of race and oppression while producing and incorporating language, theory and practice perspectives. It interrogates differences, diversity and marginalization within this core social work course and suggests implications for other professional disciplines. The discourse helps to provide insights into the ways in which power and dominance are sustained in society; the historical legacies of oppression within social work are explored. Field education is therefore implicated in these historical, socio-economic relations. While acknowledgement and consciousness of this oppression are beneficial, the text furthers the exploration by providing interventive strategies, critical understandings and ways to conceptualize issues relating to privilege and power. Since the field is about doing, critical transformative skills are included in each chapter.

The practicum in field education is the only course which is largely fulfilled at a workplace setting where students seek to integrate their theoretical skills and experiences through direct contact with clients, community development activities and policy analysis. The practicum also provides opportunities for practitioners to engage in cutting-edge theoretical discussions through their links with students and the university, and for faculty, through their liaison in the field, to engage in meaningful dialogue which acknowledges and incorporates the richness of agency-based practices in the classroom. The field education course is pivotal in many schools since it can lead to professional collaborative research partnerships on education. We live in a diverse society where we struggle with shifting global and societal challenges. The field is ideally situated for incorporating shifting changes to practice and stimulating critical thinking and dialogue about socio-political issues.

Field education, consisting of a distinct and distinguishable body of knowledge and skills, has often been described as the most critical course in the social work curriculum (Rogers 1995). In fact, policies and standards emphasize the educational and academic experiences as being rather distinct from an apprenticeship or a simple training model (Royse, Dhooper and Rompf 1999). Since there are so many constituents involved in the design and delivery of this course, it is imperative that there is accountability in every area in order to facilitate critical consciousness to a diverse society and familiarity with global social issues. The practicum or placement allows students to integrate theoretical skills, gleaned from the classroom, with life experiences, and enables them to assess their professional suitability for their respective fields of practice. There are several texts and articles which describe the many dimensions of this course ranging from administration (Kilpatrick and Holland 1993), supervision (Bogo and Vayda 1998), evaluation (Fortune and Abramson 1993) and student anxieties (Brandon and Davies 1979, Razack 2000b). This text will challenge the traditional concepts, knowledge and values of the student, educator, administrator and practitioner in order to better understand the complexities and exigencies of inclusive practice.

Although the text focuses on the practicum in social work, there are implications for other disciplines where a field experience is part of the educational requirement. In other professions the practicum may be referred to as an internship, placement or locum, while the field instructor's title could include field supervisor, practicum advisor, preceptor, supervisor or field teacher. Since this text is grounded in the belief that all parts of the system interact to facilitate an integrated change process, all constituents (for example, faculty, student, field agency, field instructor and administrators) will be included in the analysis: it is only when all participants are aware of the process, nature of intellectual inquiry and mutuality of effective learning that ongoing commitment to challenge and change will occur.

Over the past decade there has been a proliferation of articles relating to racism and oppression in social work (Lloyd 1998, Williams 1999, Dominelli 1996, Razack and Jeffery 2001). These reveal the existence of tremendous struggles, attitudinal barriers and resistance to open dialogue for an integrated change process. Domination and power continue to exert a stronghold in society: those who are marginalized still suffer harsh consequences. The field has remained largely on the periphery throughout such debates within the academy, but it is here that students formulate their knowledge base to test theories and formulate action plans for practice. Few articles focus on the area of diversity in field education, and these tend to focus on one constituent, for example, the measurement of students' attitudes about cultural diversity (Carrillo, Holzhalb and Thyer 1993).

Currently the profession of social work is said to be in a "beleaguered state"—heavily regulated and vulnerable to tensions, ambiguity and fragmentation (Taylor 1996); it is even described as having "a hole in the centre of the enterprise" (Gould and Taylor 1996). Undoubtedly, diversity and difference in a multicultural society have evoked some of these tensions, as traditional theories and practice principles are being questioned for their effectiveness and ethical dimensions. There have been efforts to include content on anti-oppression and diversity in social work curriculum and practice over the last three decades (see Garcia and Melendez 1997). Such efforts have not met ongoing challenges which continue to emerge when specific areas relating to oppression are addressed. There is still considerable resistance when the topic of racism is introduced (Razack and Jeffery 2001). However, analyses of race and oppression in the curriculum are ongoing. Although field education is a critical component of the social work curriculum, high priority has not been given to content on race and oppression. This may be the result of inadequate commitment, support and resources provided for planning, organizing and implementing the curriculum, in a way that captures the nature and spirit of anti-oppressive and antiracist field education. Facilitating an integrative change process with a critical transformative and anti-oppressive focus is highly challenging.

The world is slowly becoming more and more intimate because of our seemingly permeable borders, advanced technology and transnational exchanges. However an increase in border crossings does not mean that experiences and struggles do not persist for those who become "othered" upon entry into a country or because of skin colour, class, sexual orientation, age or ability. These markers of identity affect the way in which social issues emerge and the concomitant ways in which provision of services is affected.

The recent attacks on the World Trade Centre and retaliation efforts have created new critiques of global realities and relations. The subsequent interrogations of Muslims and Arabs, and others who happen to fit the profile of "suspected terrorists," attest to how easy it is to become the "new" group under attack. It is all the more imperative, therefore, for field educators to seek new knowledge and be aware of the current debates in order to understand how groups become targeted and labelled, and how racism and prejudice operate through global relations. At the same time it is also crucial to note how dominance and subordination are reinscribed under the guise of transformation and helping.

In field education I have observed the tendency to "manage" situations relating to diversity by an additive approach rather than one which restructures and defines integrative and inclusive pedagogical and practice principles. This text will assist in providing ways in which field education and the practicum can change to reflect a very diverse society that is constantly shifting as a result of transnational operations and shifting borders. Population diversity is not a new phenomenon. What is new are the challenges that we face with increasing flows of bodies, while the construction of knowledge remains hegemonic, with a lack of accountability and complicity about the pervasiveness of oppression for those who do not fit the dominant norms. Many first, second and third generation citizens continue to face the stigma and harshness of racism and marginalization.

This text will examine ways in which diversity and difference can be included in the curriculum of field education. A critical reflective perspective will incorporate practice initiatives. The concept of the shifting knowledge base will be used for analyzing and discussing social issues. This involves the notion that we occupy multiple and shifting identities because of our disparate locations, and evolving political and economic contexts. Critical reflective analysis will therefore be utilized to provide a way in which the material can be taken up by students, practitioners, staff and faculty to produce new meanings for practice. Marginality and difference will be discussed within an interlocking oppression framework in order to avoid reductionism and the essentializing of differences. The interlocking approach has been introduced by Hill-Collins (1990) and redefined by others (see S. Razack 1998). It works to disallow attempts to set up hierarchies in the classroom or the field and promotes a deeper level of understanding of the intensity and nature of different forms of oppression. The effectiveness of an interlocking approach depends on analyses of critical race theory as well as on the imperial historical legacies of the profession. This beginning framework will set the guidelines for interrogating other aspects of the curriculum for social work field education.

The current language of race and oppression will be discussed: resistance to this area of inquiry will be highlighted to illustrate how language can derail the process of antiracist and anti-oppression work. The political and socio-economic climate will be examined in the context of current concerns about globalization. Although administering and organizing the field can be daunting because of the time needed to negotiate excellent learning sites for every student, this process must include the space to challenge differences. This becomes the responsibility of all involved, not simply the chore of those who remain on the margins. Since the field incorporates the university, the practitioner, the student and the agency, the text will speak to the need for comprehensive changes. Thus the roles of all the constituents will be examined so that the entire process encompasses transformative practice skills. Some particular areas will be highlighted for a more detailed analysis.

The field is rife with examples of how dominant discourse continues to be sustained and how practice is also a site of privilege and exclusion. The racial minority student's voice needs to be heard, as does the voice of the person who is disabled, gay, lesbian, bisexual or "othered" because of societal stigmas. Through a systematic analysis of every aspect of the field, all voices will be heard in order to explore and uncover how the oppressor works within all of us. As I speak to these oppressor/oppressed locations, I include myself in this change process and note that, as a racial minority, straight, able faculty field coordinator, I too am implicated within these locations.

Internationalism will also be discussed, and current efforts to provide international student practica will be analyzed, since their administration and organization are a responsibility of the field office. There has been a groundswell of activities involving international fieldwork. The European Union has funded projects which are based on reciprocity between European and Western countries. The students from the North who request placement in "developing" countries face particular challenges to raise funds for travel and struggle with issues of language, culture, gender and privilege. Only those who are able to afford this experience are eligible. Students should engage in discussions about imperialism, colonization, transnationalism and renewed forms of benevolent imperialism prior to leaving for the placement. These discussions constitute ethical commitments on the part of those who wish to participate in the exchange process. A secure knowledge base is essential if these exchanges are to produce knowledge and meaning for students, faculty, host country and supervisors. Currently the exchanges appear to benefit the individual participants, but there has not been sufficient examination of the perils and merits for the profession of social work.

The text delineates the many varied constituents which comprise field education and includes some key concepts to help build an inclusive curriculum. A brief overview of core concepts of racism, oppression, colonization, imperialism and the global forces of transnationalism is critical to facilitate ongoing dialogue of antiracist and anti-oppressive perspectives for field education. Race "matters" because people perceive others as different and use these perceptions to justify unequal treatment (Fleras and Elliott 1999). It matters also because it continues to be endemic to society and has been sustained despite some efforts towards change. These perceived differences wreak havoc for minority persons in the classroom, courtroom, agency and institutions. The racialization process is evident in the way the media describes those whose skin colour and religion do not match those from dominant white Euro-Western society.

The age of imperialism represents a time when European nations conquered, plundered, colonized, exploited and stole from "developing" countries. The damage to culture and identities still lingers. Currently, imperial forces have gained momentum through the age of technology and transnationalism, which have created new approaches to global trade. These shifts allow companies and individuals to control world capital, thereby diminishing state power. Permeable borders and political unrest have resulted in waves of migration as refugees seek haven in the land of the colonizers. The treatment afforded these refugees continues during and long after their status changes to landed immigrant or citizen. For example, non-white skin colour suggests that you will probably be further down on the rung of the ladder of opportunity. These historical and present realities affect the practice of field education in social work.

Chapter 1 highlights the necessity to pay attention to critical antiracist and anti-oppressive perspectives for field education. Principles to guide a change process for the organization and management of the field are highlighted, as well as a critical examination of this powerful course. The management and coordination of the field are constant sources of tensions within the academy. These issues are underscored in Chapter 2 with a discussion of the pivotal role of the field education coordinator in the creation of a field culture in which dominance and privilege can be fully examined. In this chapter I illustrate how the field education coordinator can be marginalized in the role because of the peripheral nature of field education in the overall curriculum. The position itself is constantly under scrutiny and not accorded the status it deserves. Despite this marginalized status and the overburdened role expectations, field instructors can still pay attention to the ways in which they may be reinscribing dominance by ignoring antiracist and anti-oppressive perspectives for field education. The field education coordinator needs to first accept and understand how structural inequalities are systemic in nature and then proceed to recognize her/his own complicity within repressive structures. Students from diverse backgrounds are often challenged in their practicum; the field education coordinator needs to understand these dilemmas. A critique of whiteness is essential for many field instructors to understand their own social location. There is also an element of "niceness" which pervades this role. Since we interface with school, student and community, we need to have good interpersonal and relational skills. However this niceness also results in a task-oriented response to diversity which can exclude personal and professional exploration. The chapter highlights some of these struggles.

Funding cuts have created a devolution of services with deleterious effects on the agencies and institutions where students fulfill their practicum. Political struggles also affect the university climate. These issues are taken up in Chapter 3 with an overview of the impact of funding cuts to social services by the government of Ontario. This political analysis of the funding cuts includes the global aspect and provides an understanding of the structural elements of oppression, which impact on practice-oriented responses with clients. Chapters 4 and 5 highlight the importance of the role of the field instructor and agency in promoting and integrating antiracist and anti-oppressive field education. Tensions between the agency and university are addressed as are issues relating to racial power dynamics and knowledge production in the supervisory role. The integrative seminar is another pedagogical tool in the practicum: Chapter 6 highlights ways in which this component can strengthen inclusive field education. These seminars are usually facilitated by faculty field advisors who can create a space for students to engage in meaningful dialogue about professional identity and practice.

The needs of the students are of paramount importance in the practicum since they are the future practitioners, and developing understandings of societal issues from a socio-political perspective is imperative in their placement. Students can also risk failing the practicum for a number of reasons: some of these are highlighted in Chapter 7. Students who are from racial and sexual minority groups or are disabled, older and/or emotionally challenged face harsh realities in their environment.

The text ends with an examination of international exchanges in the practicum. While there has been increased activity within social work field departments to provide international exchange opportunities for students, there are no policies and philosophical discussions to effect international social work practice. Chapter 8 includes a critical analysis of international student exchange. This beginning study is an attempt to unsettle the international discourse and raise questions about the forces of imperialism that may be at work during and after these exchanges. The merits of exchanges are highlighted.

Chapter One

Unsettling the Field: Antiracist and Anti-oppressive Perspectives in the Social Work Practicum[1]

> The way in which groups, individuals, and ideas come to be marginalized in a given culture, society and/or place has much to do with what is considered to be knowledge and who is considered to possess it, who is perceived as knower and who as known. Clearly education is deeply implicated in these processes, which are themselves deeply implicated in the formation of identities or subject positions. (Edgerton 1993: 222)

Field education has been historically located on the periphery of social work (Schneck, Grossman and Glassman 1991). Although students report that the practicum is the most significant course in their social work program, the field has not generally been accorded full academic status (Schneck 1995). In difficult economic times the field, which demands more resources than in-class courses, can suffer from economic setbacks, and faculty and staff positions can be compromised. The field education departments in all schools of social work differ in organization and structure, although they share, as an overarching objective, the integration of knowledge, skills and experiences. The practicum course, which provides the bridge for theory and practice for students and the space to introduce new learning, can lay the groundwork for an antiracist and anti-oppressive framework for practice. Such an approach requires philosophical, organizational and methodological changes. The field is ideally located to incorporate ongoing analyses of racism and oppression because of the involvement of student, faculty, field instructor, community and agency.

Social work education is transforming to respond to the needs of a diverse society (Christensen 1995, Dominelli 1996, Longres 1991, Kolb Morris 1993). Transformation requires redressing the powerful historical legacy of oppression evident in pedagogical and practice approaches (Mullaly 1997, Pease and Fook 1999, Razack 1999a, Chau 1991, Thompson 1993, Marcoccio 1995). The practicum/field placement course is a critical nexus for this transformation—paradoxically perhaps the most critical site because of the partnerships between the university, social work practitioners and community agencies. This location provides an important opportunity to acknowledge and incorporate the specific knowledge and expertise needed for anti-oppressive social work practice in a constantly changing society. Collaborating with a range of communities, where practice involves innovative approaches with diverse groups, further informs and enriches social work education in an increasingly global context.

Internationalization is also an increasing imperative for many schools as our borders become more permeable and our societies more diverse. Transnational corporations and multinational projects dominate the economic arena, and advances in technology, trade and travel boost their power and diminish that of the state. This results in funding cuts to fragile social service programs, including health and education, as there is an urgency to compete globally. This situation, in turn, leads to increased unemployment, decentralized services, poverty and erosion of the welfare state. In the wake of these trends, the agenda to corporatize universities is more compelling and the competition for foreign capital has intensified. These market-driven trends give rise to competition and individualism: privatization is being heralded in major institutions. Social workers, educators and students face tremendous odds to battle political forces in trying to link a transnational agenda and economic public ills with private troubles. While in the classroom, students engage in political discourse to critically analyze how the social fabric gets dismantled. When they enter into a practicum they need a space to continue to examine these issues in order to incorporate a critical analysis of social issues into their training. The field practicum becomes a place where they can begin to merge their philosophy of caring with the realities of practice. For many students, whether minority or not, maintaining the political vision, especially respecting oppression, becomes a very daunting task.

This chapter focuses on how issues relating to race and oppression can be incorporated in social work field education. This analysis will be predicated on the personal challenges and ongoing efforts to develop antiracist and anti-oppressive principles for a practicum curriculum. Efforts to include antiracism and anti-oppression in social work field education discourse have been meagre at best. The first section outlines a critical perspective about antiracism and anti-oppression and provides the theoretical structure for inclusive field education. The second section details the process for change, noting the struggles and challenges which continue to arise from this ongoing commitment. The chapter concludes with implications for antiracist and anti-oppressive social work field education and practice.

A HISTORY OF NEGLECT

Discourse about the language of racism and oppression continues to be controversial. In a recent study to identify antiracist materials being utilized in schools of social work across Canada (CASSW 2000), the beginning discussion centred around language, meanings and terminology. As the study proceeded it became evident that there was no consensus on how issues, especially those relating to race and antiracism, should be addressed in curriculum and practice. At present this topic is discussed under the rubric of diversity, multiculturalism, anti-oppression and antidiscrimination. This multiplicity of terms reveals a vacuum which exists about the language and theory needed to deconstruct racism for and within social work. Race, as it relates to racism and oppression, needs to be critically examined as an integral and ongoing construct for social work (see Razack and Jeffery 2001). Studies continue to reveal the harsh effects of racism and the concomitant struggles to map out strategies for its elimination (Williams 1999). In this text race is presented as a single entity within the broader conceptualization of interlocking oppression because of its elusive but enduring nature. The insidiousness and pervasiveness of racism need to be constantly examined outside of, as well as within, the context of marginality and oppression. Racism insists on critiques of liberalism, political and economic ideology, imperialism, colonization and transnationalism. What transpires in debates about inclusive language, pedagogy and practice is an instantaneous response to flatten difference under the guise of equity and justice for marginalized groups. Such efforts restrict the analysis of race to reductionistic notions of culture, diversity and differences, without the understandings of how whites continue to benefit from privilege. Racism therefore needs to be centralized within the discourse of oppression to avoid disruption through comparison and hierarchical behaviours.

There has been a groundswell of needs assessments, studies and research that identify the imperative to infuse the social work curriculum with content relating to the oppression of marginalized groups (Dominelli 1996, Carillo, Holzhalb and Thyer 1993, CASSW 1991, Yelaja 1988). Curriculum transformation poses particular challenges for faculty, given the historical, traditional, Eurocentric theories and practice approaches (Rossiter 1995, Singleton 1994). Some articles document the need for an antiracist curriculum (Williams 1999, Macey and Moxon 1996, Dominelli 1988) and pedagogical principles to assist in developing an anti-oppressive focus (Christensen 1992, Chau 1991, Gordon 1995, Razack 1999a). Chand, Doel and Yee (1999) completed a survey to analyze the progress of antidiscriminatory practice. They found that students tended to view this approach in individualistic terms with no mention of structural concepts. Their research further indicated that students in placement seemed insecure about discussing antidiscriminatory practice for fear of "getting it wrong."

Potocky (1997) researched the effect of multicultural social work in the United States and found that there needed to be an expansion of this particular model to include responsibility and accountability for combating racism, ethnocentrism, prejudice and discrimination (323). Tully and Greene (1993) studied the coverage of articles relating to cultural diversity in social work education and reported that practice skills received greatest attention (60.4 percent), while the area most neglected related to the field practicum (1.3 percent). They pointed out the obvious anomaly that students are usually exposed to diversity in placement yet there has been minimal or no preparation for practice with respect to cultural awareness. Since 1991, when Tully and Greene's study was completed, there has been more attention to cultural diversity and antiracist practice in the literature (Dominelli 1996, Thompson 1993, Hugman 1996, Kolb Morris 1993, Van Soest 1994a). However, most of the current literature focuses on the need to understand the cultural frameworks of the clients (Insoo and Miller 1992, Christensen 1992) and the importance of ethnically sensitive social work practice (Razack, Teram and Rivera 1995, Longres 1991, Haynes and Singh 1992). Nonetheless, searches of library resources failed to identify any literature concerning the management of field education in general (Kilpatrick and Holland 1993). Literature that includes significant analysis of field education with respect to diversity and antiracism is limited to analysis of specific constituents (Van Soest 1996).

Articles and texts tend to focus on pedagogical classroom struggles, student sensitivity, cross-cultural counselling issues and theoretical understandings of racism as it pertains to immigrants and refugees. However, theories on oppression which include analyses of whiteness, privilege and power are not well-developed and integrated, and field education is not included in these analyses. Salcido and Garcia (1997) conducted an empirical study to discern the efficacy of cross-cultural training approaches. Graduate students registered for field training labs were divided into three groups and were each given a different model to learn cross-cultural knowledge and practice skills. They found that their video training model was the most successful. It is extremely difficult to evaluate the outcome of sensitivity training or a course where students learn about power and domination (Razack 1999a, Mullender 1995). Gonsales Del Valle, Merdinger, Wrenn and Miller (1991) discuss an integrated model designed for practice with a particular community. Razack, Teram and Rivera (1995) relate the process and benefits in providing placements for a few students each term in multicultural agencies. These articles focus on particular components of field education and fail to incorporate systemic and systematic change.

Rogers (1992) describes principles relating to field education and "ethnically sensitive antidiscriminatory practice." Guidelines are thus established for students to understand issues about ethnically sensitive practice. These principles, while relevant to the overall process of anti-oppression practice, neglect the pivotal role of the field department in facilitating a comprehensive anti-oppressive change approach with all the constituents. In order for the practicum to reflect the diversity in society there has to be an understanding of the importance of culture, community, race (racism) and oppression and of the need to ensure that there is a process and commitment for change and ongoing challenge.

Black, Maki and Nunn (1994) report on the difficulties of providing accurate descriptions of the relationship between field instructor and student who have different racial and ethnic backgrounds. Social workers typically identify with an image of justice and empathy and may find it particularly difficult to acknowledge and recognize their own racism and lack of understanding of antiracist social work practice. Van Dijk (1987) interprets his interviews with white Caucasians on the issue of racism:

> the better educated are just as prejudiced in their interactions, but tend to be so in a more indirect and subtle way, especially in the domains in which their own interests are perceived to be threatened ... the better educated, the elite, follow strategies of positive impression formation. Their self-image features a component of (ethnic or other forms of) "tolerance," which must be upheld especially in public, and in contacts with strangers (such as interviewers). (358)

The data further indicated that field instructors, whether minority or non-minority, discussed racial and ethnic background of clients more frequently with minority students, than did field instructors with majority students (Black et al. 1994: 15). Students with minority field instructors also stated that they were better prepared to work with clients from other ethnic groups. This research suggests that non-minority supervisors felt that they had more than adequately prepared their students to work with groups other than their own. However, the students' rating of their performance in supervision and preparation of student to work with minority groups was lower.

Given the fact that the field department has such a critical role, it is imperative that change occurs at all levels in order to ensure the delivery of a curriculum that incorporates justice, ethics and inclusion. The discussion in this chapter will highlight an antiracist and anti-oppressive framework which can be inscribed in all areas of the field education process. This chapter describes the process of attempting to ground the practicum within an anti-oppressive framework. Since the field is at the cutting edge of education and practice, the practicum must be viewed not only as a place for students to bridge theory and practice, but also as an important area to ensure that antiracist and anti-oppressive practice is actively taught. Field education can provide an important place where issues of diversity and oppression can be included in all aspects of the placement—planning, organizing, instructing and implementation. As a result, all participants—student, field instructor, agency, faculty and agency personnel—will be encouraged to address issues of difference, not simply from a cognitive approach but through discussion and practical application. The field can thus be viewed as the place where "practice can inform and reform knowledge" (Schneck 1995).

REFLECTIONS ON RACISM AND OPPRESSION

In this section I will begin with a discussion of oppression and critical race theory for social work and field education. I will ground the discussion on race in an analysis of interlocking oppression in order to examine social work's legacy of colonization, imperialism and the global forces of transnationalism.

According to Mullaly (1997), the primary focus of structural social work is oppression. Structural social work posits that oppression forms the basis of all social problems and that it is critical, therefore, to understand the dynamics and forces of oppression in order to develop transformative practice approaches. Oppression occurs because one has membership in a particular group that is deemed inferior by others in society. Oppression is systemic and endemic in society and has damaging consequences. Mullaly (1997) states that not all groups in society are oppressed and neither are people oppressed on an equal scale (139). Racism is embedded in our legal (Aylward 1999), education (Dei 1996), health and employment systems. People of colour, those with disabilities, older people, poor people, single mothers, gays and lesbians face insidious forms of discrimination. Discriminatory acts can be subtle and blatant, covert and overt, and exist at the individual, community and state levels—inherent in policies and evident in the courts and classrooms.

Young (1990) reveals a more complex conceptualization of oppression, which she reformulates into broader categories of power. She labels these as exploitation, marginalization, powerlessness, cultural imperialism and violence. She believes that oppression creates obstacles which hinder full participation in society, whether in the economic, political or cultural institutions (41). She states that public space, including that of the agency and the classroom, is not democratic. Oppression signifies a lack of economic and institutional power and is evident in our social structures. There are many people in our society who experience different forms of oppression as a result of the behaviour of those who exert their power through subordinating and excluding others. Pharr (1988) identifies common elements of oppression and the dominant societal norms that dictate rightness and righteousness by which all are to be judged. Those who do not fit are relegated to the margins. It is through this process that the "other" is created and made to feel invisible, isolated, tokenized and violated. Rodwell and Blankebaker (1992) use wounding as a metaphor to understand oppression in order to develop cross-cultural sensitivity. They provide, as an analogy, the issue of child abuse to help students understand cultural wounding.

The principles of anti-oppressive field practice are based upon an acknowledgement and understanding of prejudice, racism and oppression inherent in our traditional values and practice modalities, and the belief that action is necessary to eradicate them. This admission is necessary because social workers have been taught an essentially Euro-American model of social work, and they practise in an environment which is systematically and institutionally oppressive to a vast number of people. Some agencies have provided opportunities for reflection through workshops and conferences. However, there has not been consistent training for field instructors to facilitate reflection and discussion with students about the manifestations, historical presence and harm of prejudice, racism and discrimination. If these discussions do not occur at all levels of the placement process, the interpretation of a person's "well-being" will continue to be damaging and oppressive for students, practitioners and, more importantly, the client(s).

Oppression depends on the agents who unconsciously oppress others through their unearned privilege and benefits derived from their positions of power. Oppression is interconnected and interrelated, as each oppression needs the other in order to function: we all possess varying amounts of penalties and privilege. For example, heterosexual privilege is dependent on the subordination of lesbian women. We can occupy simultaneous oppressor and oppressed roles. In anti-oppression teaching it is not uncommon to analyze each oppression separately, creating an additive approach and, more dangerously, a hierarchical model. It is important to begin with a discussion of oppression through an overarching understanding of the complexities of its insidious nature. When there is a beginning understanding of how oppressions intersect in people's lives, we begin to understand the system of privilege, domination and subordination.

An analysis of interlocking oppression helps us to understand that groups have unequal power; therefore, voices are not heard in the same way, nor are some people spared the harsh daily effects of discrimination, racism and oppression. A historical analysis of the origins and theoretical formation of social work is necessary to understand how racism is inherent in structures and systems. If we do not critically analyze racism, colonization, imperialism and the global forces of transnationalism, the tendency is to flatten differences.

In social work there is an absence of critical race theory and language to describe and understanding oppression, marginalization, racism, imperialism and colonialism. When oppression is discussed without a critical analysis of race, the white body remains unmarked, and racism becomes a problem for *those* people and therefore *their* culture must be understood in order to assist *them* to change. While a knowledge of culture is useful, it is not enough for us to understand how racism is deployed through sociopolitical structures. Dei (1996) states that antiracism is an action-oriented strategy that addresses racism and other interlocking systems of social oppression for institutional systematic change. It names power and issues of equity and does not leave the analysis to culture and ethnic variety (252). Issues relating to competing hierarchies ignore the saliency of race and subordinate relations. Utilizing an interlocking approach to understand oppression allows for fairness and equity, since it reveals the intersectedness and connectedness of race, class, gender, ability and sexual orientation in people's lives. However, without an analysis of race as a critical entry point in the discussion of interlocking oppression, white people fail to examine the benefits they derive from the constructs of racism (Razack and Jeffery 2001). Whiteness as a construct of racism needs to be examined in order to avoid a shallow and limiting argument of oppression. Social work is intricately linked with an imperial past in terms of its origins and core Euro-American value base, This includes benevolence and caring without understanding how we reinscribe superiority by continuing to construct middle-class respectability (Razack and Jeffery 2001). These discourses of helping are not innocent of race privilege and therefore continue to sustain dominance.

The language of race in social work theory is notably absent. Critical race theory for the profession has not been discussed and race is subsumed within explications of multiculturalism, diversity, difference and antidiscriminatory approaches. Critical race theory for social work is therefore essential to understand race and oppression. In this text race and oppression are named to realize the forces of power, dominance and pervasive forms of racism. Razack and Jeffery (2001) have outlined some principles for critical race theory for social work: these principles ground the work for antiracist and anti-oppressive field education. Critical legal race theory helped to shape some of these tenets[2] (Delgado 1995, Ladson-Billings 1998).

1. Racism is normal and not an aberration in society since it is so embedded within our structures, e.g., universities, agency, institutions.

2. Storytelling is an essential process to hear and legitimize the voices of those who are marginalized through racism.

3. A critique of liberalism is necessary to deconstruct notions of incrementalism and individualism which do not account for the lack of legislation, larger structural forces and the slow process of change for people of colour.

4. An ongoing critical analysis of the field curriculum is needed to examine how issues of race are taught and to centre the analysis on power, privilege and oppression.

5. Critical race theory for social work field education insists on a knowledge of colonization, whiteness, imperialism, history, globalization and transnationalism.

6. Critical race theory for social work field education needs to be valued and recognized as an integral area of research and not be viewed as additive.

These tenets are necessary for the construction and development of antiracist and anti-oppressive field education. The focus for change should be on the needs of those who continue to be oppressed and marginalized in society and, more critically, on educator and student in order to recognize their complicity in sustaining racism and oppression and to seek transformative approaches. Field instruction should also encompass the particular needs of the minority student as well as those of the clients. The dominant ideology of inclusion and exclusion can be changed with altered contextual realities and social agency (Nagar and Leitner 1998). Although immigrants and visible minorities have a long historical presence in this country, there is still marked discrimination in practices (Seebaran and McNiven 1979). These groups tend to be disproportionately represented on caseloads within social service agencies and are the object of policies and community development projects.

A BEGINNING CHANGE PROCESS

Given the entrenched nature of racism and dominance, and the oppressive practices that result, it is imperative that the field adopt educative principles towards an antiracist and antidiscriminatory framework for practice. In this section I will highlight some of the ongoing efforts within one school of social work, recognizing the different dynamics inherent within universities. What is important is the implementation of some measure of accountability to ensure that an anti-oppressive focus is adopted in field education. I will describe initial change approaches and illustrate challenges faced along the way as well as present struggles and accomplishments.

My tenure as a faculty field coordinator began with an awareness that there had been student unrest about lack of core knowledge and content about race and oppression in the curriculum, lack of ethno-specific and innovative agencies for student placements and non-representation of faculty. Shortly after, the school decided to undertake a comprehensive curriculum review and struck a committee comprising university, student and community partners. The present curriculum reflects our philosophy of human rights, social justice, equity and inclusion. Our pedagogy is constructed within a critical perspective, and the school nourishes this approach through our course content, readings, publications and teaching. As the faculty field coordinator, I began with an exploration of ways in which ethno-specific agencies could be integral to our program and accessible for all our students.

National reviews recommend that practicum placements expand to include ethno-specific agencies (CASSW 1991) and that field instructors be knowledgeable about issues relating to diversity and oppression (CASSW 2000). In order to heed this directive and to respond to our diverse student body and a multicultural society, I invited executive directors and/or representatives from ethno-specific agencies to an inaugural meeting at the university. We outlined our goals toward inclusion in the field and listened to their need for an antiracist and anti-oppressive curriculum to prepare students to participate in their programs. Following this meeting, the Multicultural Advisory Committee," composed of members from various ethno-specific community agencies and faculty, was formed. The primary objective was for the practicum department to present an anti-oppressive framework that would result in the integration, rather than the token representation, of ethno-specific placements in our field curriculum. This approach ensures that minority and non-minority students are not simply placed at ethno-specific agencies but that an infrastructure of support and education is provided. The advisory committee members accepted field students for placement; this process allowed for feedback for change as well as agency participation in our school activities. Through a small grant we produced a video called *Beginning Inclusivity; The First Interview,* which is used as an educational tool for field education. This committee is not presently functioning, but the legacy of the work continues as I ensure representation on all our committees. We needed to meet as a separate group initially to seek input and expertise and then slowly shift towards integrative approaches.

As a result of this committee several agencies slowly began to partner with us for practicum and field education. This approach highlights the need to utilize the experts to gain access, knowledge and understanding of diverse practices at innovative agencies. In order to attract students to these non-traditional settings, we offered split placement opportunities at ethno-specific agencies for students to observe and learn about cross-cultural issues. This procedure was based on my graduate student experience, in which I was very fortunate to be the first student to begin a split placement at a multicultural agency. My experience there contrasted sharply from that of my other placements at traditional agencies (see Razack, Teram and Rivera 1995). My learning opportunities were maximized because of these varied experiences; yet the school regarded the "mainstream" supervisor as the only person qualified to evaluate my performance. In our school we agreed to shift our thinking about "formal" supervision by recognizing, respecting and valuing the qualifications, knowledge and expertise of experienced workers at these non-traditional agencies. When necessary, supervision is then augmented through consultation and collaboration with the faculty field advisor, field education coordinator and the agency. Abram, Hartung and Wernet (2000) discussed an enhanced field project model which included the non-M.S.W. task supervisor, the student and the M.S.W. field instructor. This model would serve schools where there is inflexibility in allowing non-M.S.W. supervisors to evaluate and supervise students. I have found that innovative agencies (e.g., multicultural ones and those which serve specialized populations) provide us with opportunities to partner in unique ways about education. However they pose challenges for the academy and accrediting bodies because many of the workers lack acceptable Western-standard qualifications. Schools need to seek and preserve these sites since the expert knowledge of these workers is sorely needed for work with a diverse clientele. The popularity among students of such placements will grow, both as a result of the diverse learning experiences provided and of the global approaches to education. The likelihood that social work graduates will be hired by these agencies is an added incentive.

The practicum committee, consisting of faculty, students, staff and practitioners, serves an important function in promoting the objectives of antidiscriminatory practice. This committee should be representative of a diverse community in order to validate and include different voices and varied perspectives. This committee assists with the production of our practicum newsletter, *Field View:* this medium is another tool to incorporate diversity. Faculty, visiting professors, field instructors and students are encouraged to write articles; innovative and international placements and field events are also highlighted. Since this newsletter demands time and energy, it does increase the workload of the already burdened field department. We have not managed to produce these newsletters consistently because of our ongoing expansion and workload. Many of these initiatives can easily be incorporated into any existing structure despite the differences in student bodies regarding numbers, diversity or approach.

Our written material and forms reflect our commitment to diversity: the practicum manual has been significantly revised to include an anti-oppressive focus. Shifting significantly from a distinct clinical focus, evaluation and progress reports reflect traditional and non-traditional practice approaches. The field department also reflects diversity in terms of staffing. These changes emphasize our commitment to, and acceptance of, traditional and non-traditional practice in a diverse society. It is imperative that the department regards field education as a vital component of the curriculum. Recognizing the pivotal role of the field is essential in creating an infrastructure to facilitate an anti-oppressive framework for practice.

THE ROLE OF THE STUDENT

Through our revised curriculum, students have generally been exposed in the classroom to material about diversity, identity, antidiscriminatory practice, power and bureaucracy within the organization. Many also have personal and professional exposure to challenging oppression and racism. There are several ways to ensure that students achieve antiracist and anti-oppressive perspectives in the practicum. All students attend a practicum orientation seminar which covers a wide range of topics including innovative learning at non-traditional agencies and the importance of thinking and working cross-culturally. Weeks (1981) elaborated on the merits of placements at innovative settings:

> Field placements in innovative community settings involve maintaining broad boundaries for social work practice. They offer students alternatives to therapeutic work with individuals and families.... They allow group work, community development and organizing to be central rather than peripheral social work methods.... Advocacy ... and systems brokerage are considered as valuable and important as counselling and therapy. (7)

Students need to understand bureaucratic structures and be able to work effectively in these settings while learning to critically reflect on practice. In this way they will acquire an analysis that goes beyond application of a learnt theory for a particular situation (Goldstein 1993). There is currently a radical shift in practice approaches as traditional clinical settings are being challenged to embrace community perspectives and link families with resources. Practicum graduates are invited to these orientation seminars to share their placement experiences and their learning of anti-oppression principles for practice. These seminars occur in most schools and are an ideal place to remind students of inclusive practice.

A discussion of anti-oppressive principles is also important during the students' pre-screening interview with the field coordinator to determine strengths, areas of interest and potential placement choices. Forms for students are revised on an ongoing basis to reflect changes in the social service environment. Practicum students must attend integrative seminars each term with their faculty field advisor. The seminars provide a further mechanism for those students who do not have opportunities at their placement to effectively begin to question the exclusionary nature of practice (see Chapter Six). Students are encouraged to critically analyze the organizational structure of their placement agency and share their challenges in working with a diverse population. It is hoped that all students who have been involved in courses relating to anti-oppression and who attended orientation seminars, interviews and other meetings in preparation for the field will feel more able to discuss practice issues with a diverse population at a pre-screening meeting and also during their placement at the agency.

ONGOING CHALLENGES AND STRUGGLES

There are ongoing system changes in the approach, design, implementation, process and structure of field education within all schools. It is imperative to relate ongoing struggles as well as celebrate the strengths. The field department in any school constantly works with reduced resources and administrative support. While agencies are shrinking and access for students is limited, the university is forced to expand and accept more students. Over the past few years we have greater numbers both in the B.S.W. and the M.S.W. program. All our graduate students complete a practicum during the course of their study. These changes have stretched the department as we seek to balance the daily tasks of actually locating and negotiating learning sites with our inherent philosophy of inclusivity and anti-oppressive practice.

Last fall a practicum task force was struck to examine our present structure in order to ensure that we were living up to our mission statement of promoting inclusive practice. This committee consisted of a diverse group who very carefully examined our current practices and procedures and made recommendations for change. One student conducted a thorough study of students' evaluation of the practicum forms and noted areas of concern (Preston 1999). The result of the evaluations indicate that students valued highly their learning and enriched practicum experiences. Some concerns were expressed about the faculty field role and the nature and purpose of integrative seminars. These concerns will be examined further in the text.

SOME IMPLICATIONS FOR SOCIAL WORK EDUCATION

This field education model is described from personal and professional perspectives but with a recognition of its adaptability. It is the result of an ethical and moral need to integrate an anti-oppressive approach in the practicum. It seems illogical to wait for the academy to fully reflect antiracist and anti-oppressive pedagogical principles in the classroom in order to influence changes in the field. The incorporation of an anti-racist/ anti-oppressive curriculum is arduous and still not a priority for many educators and practitioners who are fearful and resistant to this kind of change. The classroom effectively remains a private domain and comes up for public scrutiny only through occasional evaluations.

In social work there are challenges to the traditional power differential between the lecturer and student, and, more importantly, between the social worker and the client. There are also many workshops about the power dynamics in field instruction, which speak to the imbalance of power between the student and field instructor (Rogers 1992). These issues demand ongoing reflection and discussion from personal and professional standpoints, especially since they highlight the daily reality of oppression and subordination.

Moffatt (1994) discusses a reflective process whereby the social work student can reach "an understanding of a persons' well-being in practice." This process assumes that the student/worker will be able to recognize oppressive behaviours and be reflective in order to understand the other. However, if, within the student/field instructor realm of education and experiences, there has been little or no focus on racism and anti-oppressive principles, how then can these "persons well-being" be understood? What is the mechanism provided for student/instructor discourse about oppressive practice? It becomes critical, therefore, to provide the structure and space for honest reflections and dialogues about oppression. The field education process, in contrast to the traditional classroom, provides different and significant opportunities for the introduction of material related to oppression in critical discussion with all its constituents—student, faculty, field instructor, administration, agency and community.

Freire (1970) refers to the common approach to pedagogy, the "banking" concept, in which education is carried out by teacher *for* learner or by teacher *about* learner. He contrasts this to the teacher working *with* the learner "mediated by the world—a world which impresses and challenges both parties, giving rise to views or opinions about it" (82). Working with the learner is vital in field instruction for facilitating discussions of sensitive issues. Social work is viewed as a caring and helping profession. In today's society, social work educators are struggling to educate and prepare students for the realities of practice. I have often challenged the "given" in social work that empathy should be enough when working with clients. I know that empathy does not generally facilitate a discussion about oppression, and, even if this discussion happens, it is only in the context of being empathic relative to the given situation and not through an examination of the political implications of imperialism, colonialism or racism. If the field instructor has been trained to listen, acknowledge pain and give corrective feedback without an analysis that includes attention to systemic inequalities, then this may result in further disservice to the student and client.

The field department simply cannot afford to maintain a peripheral position in the curriculum because of the availability of opportunities through the links with all areas of the profession. The structure for change is permissible, affordable, attainable and sustainable. Field coordinators and faculty need to advocate the importance of the position and the role of field instruction in order to first acquire the commitment to change. Innovation and enthusiasm are important elements to sustain efforts and create commitment. Inviting the community to collaborate, sit on school council and search committees, and participate in meetings and other important functions gives the department prominence and encourages a wide degree of participation. There are numerous opportunities for critical reflection and inquiry about themes relating to oppression, racism, colonialism and the resulting marginalization of groups. The framework presented in this chapter has generated many research projects which are critical to field education. The field can make concrete and practical adjustments; the process of change can then be documented for research and scholarship purposes. The field then *administers* and simply *does* and becomes a critical area where "practice can reform knowledge."

CONCLUSION

Anti-oppression principles deserve ongoing debate, challenge and collaboration. The integration of these principles requires particular attention in the development of the practicum. This development needs to be documented and evaluated for teaching and practice purposes since there is no model to fully eradicate oppressive practices. Anti-oppressive practice needs to include introspection and private inner confrontation: it must also be compelling enough to brave interactive discourse, admission of vulnerabilities and cultural wounding.

Goldstein (1993) points out that "any serious changes in field education would significantly disturb and even alter all other aspects of the curriculum" (181). The approaches outlined in this chapter have significantly transformed the practicum department but need to be continuously monitored, evaluated and challenged to reflect diversity and difference. Each division of field education needs to play a critical role in anti-oppression/antiracist analysis in order to reflect inclusivity and appreciation of differences. This anti-oppressive framework incorporates the roles of students, field instructors, faculty, community and administrators in institutional and systemic change processes. The role of the field education coordinator is integral to the field education process.

NOTES

1. The author has previously developed some of these ideas in "Anti-oppressive Social Work: A Model for Field Education." In Gwat-Yong Lie and David Este (eds.) 1999.
2. For further analysis of these tenets, see Razack and Jeffery 2001.

Chapter Two

Niceness, Whiteness and Oppression:
The Role of the Field Education Coordinator

> a key but lonely role ... no one has greater impact and no one is
> more isolated ... a special lot ... a unique blend of educator–
> administrator ... struggling to keep ... in synchrony the needs of
> faculty, students and community agencies. (Hawthorne and
> Holtzman 1991: 326)

The role of the field education coordinator is pivotal to every aspect of
field education. The practicum constitutes about one-third to half of the
curriculum in many schools; the tasks of building and ensuring that there
are excellent and sustainable field education sites, training and educational
seminars for field instructors and students, adequate linkages with faculty
and agency personnel, amid a host of other duties, rest with the field
education coordinator. The workload is vast in scope and labour-intensive.
The role comprises educative and administrative responsibilities and this
duality, as will be illustrated, can lead to reduced status and influence
within the academy. There is significant vulnerability inherent in this
position because of the shifting contexts within the administration as well
as at professional agencies and institutions. Resources are usually insufficient to adequately fulfill the diverse array of duties which demand year-
long labour. There is an urgency for this role to be redefined within the
profession in order for the work to be recognized in its entirety despite
differences relating to titles, job description and the often oppressive
nature of the position. This is especially important because of the crucial
role field coordinators are able to play in setting the tone for antiracist and
anti-oppressive field education. Examining this aspect of the role will be a
key feature of this chapter.

  I begin with a discussion of the scope of this role and include some of
the pitfalls inherent in the structure and design of the position. The
traditional role of the field instructor, including its challenges and oppor-

tunities to effect change, will be highlighted together with an outline of the duties and functions. These details contextualize how this position should be embraced and organized within the institution and provide some guidelines for field coordinators who envision commitment to inclusive field education. The support systems to facilitate this perspective will be delineated, together with a discussion of the skills, qualifications, experience and knowledge base befitting this position. An examination of whiteness, privilege, power and dominance is crucial to ensure that field education coordinators understand and embrace antiracist and anti-oppressive perspectives in all areas which comprise field education. The coordinator helps shape practice by ensuring that students have excellent and challenging learning sites to enhance their skills, debate differences and increase knowledge, all of which will strengthen their professional identity. It is imperative to recognize that excellence in field education also includes antiracist and anti-oppressive principles.

CRITICAL MEANINGS AND SIGNIFICANCE OF THIS ROLE

According to Schneck (1995), field education coordinators are in an enviable position "to evaluate and provide practice innovation for social work services and methods" (9). We sense the pulse of the community more so than our other colleagues since we witness the way a political agenda influences the climate of the agency. This in turn affects placements. We interface with the faculty, students, agencies and many other professional bodies and we have access to a wealth of professional colleagues in the community with whom we can create alliances and collaborations for education. We enjoy their trust and we earn credibility through our skillful negotiations in establishing learning sites for students. We can tap into this reservoir of community contacts to create projects, evaluate programs and research critical social issues. Since the practicum is a substantial component of the curriculum we can integrate this knowledge of the community to influence education and practice.

We have rich resources through our links with field education coordinators locally, nationally and internationally. With advances in technology these connections are made instantaneous through electronic mail. This provides an immediate support group and network of colleagues with whom to share ideas and responses to questions on every aspect of field education. I have been impressed with the network of field coordinators who meet annually at the Canadian Association of Schools of Social Work, Congress of Social Sciences and Humanities Conference in Canada. Here

I witness how committed this group is to field education and to providing collegial support. In our packed agenda we identify tasks, promote and analyze our multiple roles and the demands of the position and ponder the rigours and complexities of social work field education. The coordinators do not get mired in discussions of their own oppressive work conditions but rather they share varied approaches and innovative ideas to accomplish their multifarious tasks. We keep abreast of policies and accreditation standards which affect the field and lobby for changes when needed. We have demanded representation on the board of directors of our national association. When there are ongoing pedagogical and practice struggles and concerns which require attention through research, committees are easily struck to conduct surveys and small studies. There is also an innovative committee of field educators in the U.S.: scholarship relating to field education is promoted and valued through symposia and presentations at their annual conference. Many international scholarly conferences on field education are emerging.

The field education coordinator acts as the link with the community, is the ambassador of the school and has to be efficient and knowledgeable, not only about the field but also about the academic curriculum and professional practice. She/he has to be able to understand and work with the entire student body, possess sound interpersonal skills and be an effective public speaker. The coordinator needs to profile all aspects of the profession. It is inappropriate for the coordinator to indicate publicly a preference for a particular practice area since agencies and students incorporate a varied and diverse range of professional practice approaches. An understanding of the exigencies of micro-, mezzo- and macro-social work is essential to ensure that all aspects of the program incorporate an antiracist and anti-oppressive framework for practice. The latter task is most feasible in this position because there are ample opportunities to facilitate inclusivity and many constituents with whom to engage for meaningful change.

Field education coordinators can develop practice paradigms to respond to the challenges facing society. As a field coordinator I am acutely aware of the trends in social services which directly impact on social work education. The field coordinator can provide feedback about these shifts in practice to the school at curriculum reviews, faculty meetings and instruction seminars. However, the inherent strengths, opportunities and dynamism of this role can get easily repressed and diminished because of some of the oppressive realities befalling this particular position. What can be a strength can easily become a pitfall when there are a devaluation of the role, insufficient resources and an unsupportive administrative structure.

ENDURING THE STRUGGLES

The role of the field education coordinator is rife with conflict and struggles. I will begin with the name/title which varies considerably and can be a source of tension. One can be referred to as the field education coordinator, practicum coordinator, director of field education, academic field coordinator or practicum liaison. The diversity of titles exists because there is no consensus regarding the status and benefits accorded this particular position. Titles are also contentious when there are attempts to undermine the complexities and importance of the role. Thus the use of the term "director," "liaison" or "coordinator" can reflect internal power dynamics between faculty and administration rather than the relatedness of the educative and administrative elements of this position.

No matter what the title, field education coordinators occupy marginal status within schools of social work, and workload is a constant concern. The role in itself is oppressive because of its inherent lack of influence. According to Hawthorne and Holtzman (1991), at the beginning of their tenure, field directors typically identify themselves primarily as educators. However, over time, they discover that the role becomes increasingly administrative. This can result in lack of support, communication, and opportunities for innovative field development. Because field coordinators often feel undervalued in their position, job satisfaction can waver, especially when there are ongoing changes to the tasks and responsibilities (Hawthorne and Holtzman 1991). In the wake of restructuring, downsizing and cutbacks, the field coordinator often suffers as rank becomes tenuous, titles change and resources are reduced. If the school is facing restrictions with hiring, the position of faculty field coordinator may become endangered and in jeopardy of being reassigned professional or managerial status.

The field curriculum needs to be specialized within schools so that the duality of education/administration is understood by all. Kilpatrick and Holland (1993) note these dilemmas in their study of the management of the field instruction program in social work. They describe the conflict inherent in the role between the administrative demands of directing and coordinating field education. The traditional expectations in academia regarding publishing, teaching and research, which are required to fulfill tenure and promotion requirements, are also problematic. As a faculty field education coordinator, I have certainly felt that the expectations for my tenure and promotion, especially in the area of scholarly publications, have not been clearly delineated. Many faculty field coordinators have to leave their positions in order to secure the time needed for research and publishing. The fear that a tenure and promotion committee will not recognize the educational aspects of field education is real: in my own case, field experience was not accepted in my academic profile without a query.

The majority of faculty field coordinators are not expected to teach and conduct research. Some are named as faculty lecturers with no expectation of research. Many coordinators simply occupy professional and managerial status in their institution. I recently conducted a poll of tenured/tenure-track faculty field coordinators on our national listserve: only four out of a potential thirty-six responded. This suggests that very few field coordinators in Canada have faculty positions and that the field practicum course is undervalued. Although I do not feel that those with professional and managerial positions are not effective in their role, I do view field education as being so pivotal to social work that there needs to be academic recognition of its educational nature. How this recognition is accomplished may be up to the individual school, but there ought to be some strong national standards which should be strictly adhered to by accreditation bodies. In a recent study McChesny (1999) unexpectedly found that field education directors lacked knowledge about national programs; that orientation and training programs are strengthened when there is improved networking among directors; and that a comprehensive national training curriculum was greatly needed.

Unfortunately the coordinator's role has traditionally been viewed by many faculty as an administrative one. The organization and management of the field indisputably require excellent administrative and organizational skills to be able to fulfill many of the tasks. However the success of this administration depends on an ongoing knowledge base of social work, more specifically current socio-political trends and practice issues which affect the field on a daily basis. This knowledge cannot be gained by focusing solely on the administrative elements of field education. Knowing what to teach at field instruction seminars, how to plan and deliver orientation seminars and developing and effecting field education demand much more than organizational and administration skills. Some schools have rotating faculty members who provide the training for field instructors. While this approach can serve to emphasize the academic nature of the field, it can also be viewed as adding academic components entirely divorced from the field department. There may not be any effort to consult the field education coordinator about the pressing needs in the community and the socio-political realities within agencies. Some faculty members may not be sufficiently aware of practice issues to conduct this training of field instructors. A review of the literature indicates that many of the problems outlined here have historical roots and continue to be a source of angst, especially for field education coordinators (Moore 2000, Goldstein 1993, Kilpatrick and Holland 1993).

Another area which deserves more attention is the area of research and scholarship in field education. Since the roles of field education coordinator do not include research and scholarship expectations, these goals must be pursued in addition to their heavy administrative and teaching demands. As a result, pedagogy and academic concerns are not pursued extensively and rigorously. The field has historically been accorded minimal attention in the literature: issues relating to race and oppression have not been extensively covered (Tully and Greene 1993). Most field literature focuses on the educational and administrative structures and technological aspects of the delivery of field education (Fortune and Abramson 1993, Bogo and Vayda 1998). Research about the placement process, learning styles, evaluation surveys and computer technology has been the norm (Rompf, Royse and Dhooper 1993, Salcido, Garcia, Cota and Thompson 1995, Choy et al. 1998, Cooper and Briggs 2000). Other articles describe student sensitivity, personal struggles in the field, confidentiality and legal issues, the "problem" student, performance evaluations, students with disability, at-risk situations, and safety and security issues (Schneck 1995: 7–8). While these areas continue to be important to the vision of excellence in field education, there needs to be critical research into the daunting daily task of advancing critical antiracist and anti-oppressive practice. A typical response to the issue of diversity is to provide sporadic cross-cultural sensitivity training. Perry (2001) warned of the dangers of only studying the "other" and felt that important insights must be gained by paying more attention to the white majority (86). It is not enough for us to focus only on training students to be ethnically sensitive and to understand different cultures.

The field is ideally situated to understand the exigencies of practice in tandem with the curriculum in order to discern where struggles lie and critical changes can be made. According to Schneck (1995),

> Academic researchers and policy makers yearn for the relevance and credibility provided only in "the real world." And practitioners in a very demanding time seek sources of consultation and value fresh perspectives. (9)

The field education coordinator is ideally located to engage in many practice-based research initiatives because of the extensive links with the community. The socio-political vision of a diverse society and its impact on the practice of social work are at the heart of social work field education. These issues must be of primary concern to the field education coordinator: ongoing knowledge of ways to effect this holistic approach to field education should be a major goal. At this juncture I will highlight ways to ensure that repressive structures do not limit the potential of this critical position in social work.

CRITICAL APPROACHES FOR FIELD EDUCATION COORDINATION

Kilpatrick and Holland (1993) conducted a study on the management of field instruction programs in social work education and found that faculty commitment is key to the success of the program. They highlight the value of the academic faculty field education role and state that there should be non-tenure positions for the many day-to-day administrative tasks. They emphasized that the role needs to be redefined to make it a tenure-track position as is the case with other academic administrative positions. The field education coordinator's position would be more secure, instead of being under constant scrutiny, especially in times of major cutbacks and fiscal restraints. A field education colleague from Australia stated that her department hires three full-time staff with graduate social work degrees to organize and manage the field. Because she acts as the academic director, she can obtain substantial grants to conduct agency and institutionally based research on the field. This research usually has an interdisciplinary focus. At this university the practicum is therefore fully integrated into the curriculum and the school.

Field education coordinators need to unite in order to present a powerful voice about the nature and importance of field education. Some field colleagues fear that if there is legislation requiring field directors to be a faculty members, the professional and managerial positions will be eliminated. On the contrary, it can be argued that there will always be the need for a strong administrator as well as a dynamic academic director. Both positions require social work education, skills and expertise. Several studies with a national scope have examined the role of coordinators; however, they have been conducted with limited resources and were hindered by the difficulty of measuring and allotting a specific time value to the vast array of duties inherent in the role. An extensive, in-depth research project needs to be undertaken to clearly identify the expectations of the field course, the resources and staffing needs, and the relative priorities of research, teaching and publishing for field educators.

Field coordinators need to remain at the cutting edge in terms of knowledge of social issues in the profession. Social work field training is constantly undergoing change—currently many shifts result from trends toward managed care and competencies (Rossiter 2001). In this era of cutbacks and economic constraints, Jarman-Rohde et al. (1997) indicate that field directors should collaborate with other schools of social work, colleges and agencies to enrich networks and strengthen effectiveness especially through the sharing of vital resources.

ANTIRACISM AND ANTI-OPPRESSIVE APPROACH

Together with their extensive duties, it is also imperative that field education coordinators pay attention to their role in integrating an antiracist and anti-oppressive perspective in every aspect of field education. I have written elsewhere about the ways in which an anti-oppressive model can be introduced within field education (see Razack et al. 1995). Others have described ways to include cross-cultural and anti-oppressive approaches to field education (Gonsales Del Valle, Merdinger, Wrenn and Miller 1991, Salcido, Garcia, Cota and Thompson 1995). What I and the rest have not focused on are the critical responsibilities of the field education coordinators to effect an overall inclusive approach.

The epistemology of anti-oppression is a very detailed and shifting area of study. As earlier stated, the field education coordinator works within oppressive structures. In turn the field education coordinator can also be oppressive if there is not considerable effort to incorporate antiracist and anti-oppressive perspectives. This responsibility cannot be compromised even in the face of cutbacks and restraints. It is our moral and ethical duty to be knowledgeable about race, racism and oppression in order to shift the curriculum of social work field education. Field education coordinators need to understand what constitutes inclusive and anti-oppressive practice and work to incorporate this approach within the many areas of the field. This knowledge base of the field education coordinator is essential for organizing and administering all aspects of the practicum.

RACISM AND OPPRESSION

The first step in being able to effect this approach is a critical, unproblematic belief that there are structural, systemic and systematic injustices and inequities deeply embedded in society. Racism, homophobia, classism, ableism and ageism are but a few of the manifestations of these injustices. Each of these areas demands a comprehensive analysis and study in order to examine the prevailing forces of power and dominance.

Second, field education coordinators need to understand their own location within privilege and subordination. We work within repressive structures and are therefore implicated in sustaining dominance and dominant ideology (Carty 1993). If the field education coordinator shrugs off the responsibility of unearthing inner prejudices, privilege and power, and is innocent of the impact of these on students and others, then the first step towards fulfilling an anti-oppressive agenda in the school will entail mere lip service.

Third, anti-oppression strategies do not only translate into finding a few ethno-specific agencies and conducting a seminar occasionally on cross-cultural practice. What has to shift is the belief of the coordinator that this perspective needs to pervade the field curriculum. This shift begins with knowledge of the self.

WHITENESS, PRIVILEGE AND SUBORDINATION

It is my observation from attending many field education coordinators' meetings that whiteness pervades this role. Not many field education coordinators are persons of colour or obviously from other marginalized groups. The role is largely filled by women: my assumption is that most are heterosexual. Gender, race, sexual orientation and class issues intersect therefore to profile the status of the field education coordinator. Our accreditation standards insist that there be recognition of diversity in the field. However, in practice, the response to this requirement tends to be a task-centred one. Efforts to incorporate an anti-oppressive agenda tend to be additive and prescriptive and do not attempt to examine the underlying structure which sustains oppression. "Managing diversity" becomes the task at hand, and efforts to recruit some ethno-specific agencies to respond to accreditation standards become the norm. As Blommaert and Verschueren (1998) state:

> The management paradigm which dominates the debate on diversity, ignores its status as a simple fact of life. In other words, the debate itself turns diversity into a problem to be managed.... It is clearly dominated by the (powerful) majority, to such an extent that minority members are not even allowed to participate. "Management" is always in the hands of the powerful, and the manage-

ment of diversity is not an exception.... Therefore the debate is really about the "other" as an object of discourse. (15)

This externalizing approach denies complicity in sustaining oppression. Examining internal beliefs in order to grapple with the intricacies of race and oppression is largely avoided and viewed as an impediment to an already cumbersome role. A beginning discussion is therefore necessary to examine our location and complicity within dominant structures (see S. Razack 1998).

The issue of whiteness within the field deserves critical attention. Frankenberg (1993) states that race shapes white women's lives in the same way as gender, class, sexual orientation and ability. White people do live racially structured lives and this needs to be recognized on an individual level if accountability and change are to occur. According to Frankenberg (1997),

whiteness ... is a set of linked dimensions ... is a location of structural advantage, of race privilege ... is a "standpoint," a place from which white people look at ourselves, at others, and at society ... [it] refers to a set of cultural practices that are usually unmarked and unexamined. (211)

Through an examination of whiteness, field educators can begin to examine how the "other" is viewed racially in our traditional discourse. Perry (2001) conducted interviews with white students who expressed that their racial identity was cultureless. While recognizing the discourse about "white culture" (Roediger 1994), Perry states that whites exert power when "'claiming they have no culture" (59). I would argue that claiming culturelessness and opting for a colour-blind position can also unintentionally maintain superiority.

Recognizing the systemic and institutional nature of racism and oppression within the academy and at agencies is critical for challenge and change. It is therefore very important for field education coordinators to note how embedded racism is within society and how their lives are shaped by it. Re-examining personal history is also necessary to unlearn assumptions; we need to use an anti-imperialist lens to halt the aversion inherent in the gaze of the "other." Too often the work of changing structures begins from an external social location without conceptual understandings of how "responses to subordinate groups are socially organized to sustain existing power arrangements " (S. Razack 1998: 8). We cannot rid ourselves and society of oppression unless we continuously locate ourselves within our history.

Since field education coordinators are so inundated with day-to-day activities and demands, personal reflection on issues relating to race and oppression may not be seen as a priority. However, it is our moral responsibility to apply the same expectations of excellence to ourselves that we do to our students: if we ourselves are unaware of the damage of racism, homophobia, classism, ageism and ableism from personal and professional standpoints, then we are not being effective and morally responsible in our role. Our students may hesitate to discuss potential risks they face in the practicum if we do not provide a positive space (Razack 2000b, Messenger and Topal 1997). Contradictory approaches to race and oppression are inherent in schools of social work where efforts for change are met with struggles and resistance about language and academic freedom (Razack and Jeffery 2001). Since field coordinators work within repressive structures, they must be creative in organizing for change with limited support.

Students of colour may need to discuss their fears and anxieties with the coordinator in order to locate an anti-oppressive setting. Gay, lesbian and bisexual students are aware of hostile terrains in the field and often remain closeted in order to avoid risks and marginality (Messenger and Topal 1997). Students with disability face daily forms of oppression: the field is especially challenged to provide them with adequate learning sites (Bial and Lynn 1995). Their pain can be intense: if we do not build a positive space to allow for liberated discussions, our service and role are compromised. As field coordinators we need to work towards eliminating barriers and ensuring that our agencies and field instructors grasp the intricacies of structural forms of oppression. We need to accept that understanding begins within the self before we can facilitate change perspectives for our field constituents. The social construction of whiteness and the concomitant power and privilege that are accorded many because of privileged social location need to be understood so that we are not innocent of our own complicity in sustaining oppression. Field coordinators have not focused on issues of whiteness and privilege, and analyses of power are usually limited to supervisor/student relationships (Bogo and Vayda 1998) rather than on interrogation of the self in the provision of field education. Maybe these omissions result from the powerlessness, marginalization and subjugation endemic in the position.

There is also an element of "niceness" that is a central expectation of the field education coordinator's role. It arises partly out of the necessity of negotiating the complex networks and constituents encountered on a daily basis. The interactions with faculty, students, administrators, agency personnel and practitioners require tact, diplomacy and "niceness." This response could mask our role in sustaining racism and oppression. For example, when placements break down the field education coordinator has to be sensitive and diplomatic in responding to both student and field instructor. As a minority faculty field educator I have hesitated to voice issues relating to race and our obligation to recognize and respond to our own location within racist structures. It is often easier for us to externalize the debates about diversity and difference by presenting seminars about sensitivity and cross-cultural training than it is for us to examine ourselves.

At times I can intuitively recognize the forces of racism and oppression from the telling and witnessing of stories about a particular difficulty in the practicum. There are usually subtle underlying forms at play which are complicated and difficult to challenge immediately. Often it is necessary to return to the particular situation after the student has completed the placement or when the student has been successfully placed elsewhere. These situations are not ideal because any discussion of race and oppression can degenerate into perceived attacks on personal flaws, accompanied by anger, guilt and "institutional white defensiveness." The field educators should therefore be knowledgeable and fairly skilled in discussing the systemic and oppressive nature of the institution in ways which will allow dialogue and reflection towards change. Tensions and anxieties also emerge between faculty and field agencies (Witkin 1998). The element of "niceness" can emerge in these interactions and act as a mask to avoid dealing with the harshness of discrimination and oppression, as well as an inhibitor to discussing how colonization, transnationalism, imperialism and other forms of societal inequities shape the lives of many of our students and impact on all aspects of the field.

SOME REFLECTIVE RESPONSES TO RACISM AND OPPRESSION

The field coordinator must recognize the need to change dominant structures, and this commitment should be reflected in personal and professional behaviours. As stated earlier, field education is in a constant state of flux mainly because of the historical lack of recognition of its importance to the curriculum (Kilpatrick and Holland 1993). During the first year of my tenure on a limited contractual term, discussions of the field position resulted in a change to a tenure-track appointment with open competition. This shift signified more status and credibility to the role of field education within the university and in the wider community. This appointment came on the heels of program reviews which emphasized the need for more student placements at ethno-specific agencies to be integrated into the program. It was apparent that fundamental change to the field department and to the school was needed in order to deliver a program based on anti-oppression principles. Similar efforts to extend cultural diversity to field education have been noted in other schools. Razack et al. (1995) describe the process involved in providing one day multicultural placements for a few students in a graduate program. Courses about cultural diversity provided students with a framework for sensitive practice (Rogers 1992, Salcido et al. 1995).

Field education has to ensure accountability in every area to reflect a view of justice, rights and inclusivity. The role of the field education coordinator is crucial in guiding this process and ensuring that key players in the delivery of this course adhere to these principles. The field program, if done well, can add to the culture, climate and perception of the school by other academics and the community. The field can convey the message of anti-oppressive practice through the students, the links with the agency and field instructor; it can shift the norms of practice. The liaison of the faculty field advisor is essential to this process. If the school does not pay enough attention to the academic nature of field education, it is easy to slip into the role of locating a few ethno-specific and innovative field placement agencies to respond to oppression and maintain accreditation standards. A model of linking the school practicum with ethno-specific agencies was implemented in one school and, although there were individual benefits to the student, the academic institution was largely left untouched since it appeared so external to the field program and the university (Razack, Teram and Rivera 1995). This additive model continues to reinscribe dominant behaviours and ideology. It is important, therefore, for the field coordinator to first understand what constitutes anti-oppressive and antiracist practice. This knowledge base constitutes important criteria for organizing and administering all aspects of the practicum. If the field educational coordinator's role is limited to finding appropriate placement sites with agencies whose policies and commitment to anti-oppressive practice fit with the curriculum, then field education will not encompass all that it is mandated to accomplish. Likewise if the field education coordinator does not have an inherent belief system and knowledge about oppression, privilege, power, whiteness, imperialism and colonization then the entire student body and field program will reflect these gaps in knowledge. Minority voices will therefore be silenced (Razack 2001).

If the field education coordinator engages in a self-reflective process to become more knowledgeable about racism and oppression, the field department will reflect this approach through the staffing, written material and educative seminars and forums. The agencies will know that the department is serious in its efforts to combat injustice and that oppressive and racist behaviours and practices will not be tolerated. However, some organizations can also foster and encourage passive forms of racism and discrimination, especially if attempts are made to avoid dealing with tensions in the field. Some of these conflicts occur when we receive feedback from students who are concerned that the staff is completely white and the client population very diverse, or that the supervisor engages in discriminatory behaviour and explains it as a result of stress. Often we do not respond appropriately to these charges because of fear that agencies will respond by withholding placements or because there is no space provided to discuss contentious issues. The scarcity of appropriate and popular placements thus contributes to sustaining dominance. This scenario can be reversed if field education coordinators understand how power and dominance are inscribed and take action to prevent this outcome. Field education coordinators are also responsible for organizing and facilitating orientation seminars and conducting interviews with students. These learning opportunities should include analyses of differences, diversity, race and oppression to ensure that the practice agencies have a critical understanding of these issues.

In summary, some of the ways in which coordinators can ensure that the field education course maintains anti-oppressive and antiracist perspectives are as follows:

- understand, accept and educate oneself in the area of race and oppression;
- be aware of one's own complicity in sustaining dominance and privilege where applicable and work towards eradication;
- understand how power operates and is organized within institutions and within self;
- be accountable in engagements with minority and non-minority students;
- be instrumental in defining clearly delineated roles and functions for the field education coordinator and the constituents;
- ensure that seminars have an integrated analysis of power, race and oppression;
- ensure that staff in innovative, traditional and non-traditional place-

ments understand and accept the school's approach;
- ensure that policies and procedures reflect an anti-oppressive knowledge base;
- liaise with a range of agencies and try to visit non-traditional and innovative settings to partner in field education;
- provide liberated spaces in which to dialogue about ongoing political issues, e.g., integrative seminars;
- incorporate a research agenda which will advance the scholarship of field education;
- include a practicum report and discussion at every faculty meeting;
- ensure that the practicum department reflects diversity wherever feasible, e.g., in staffing;
- ensure that evaluation forms, manuals, correspondence, guidelines, etc. reflect inclusivity.

CONCLUSION

This chapter highlights the complex role of the field education coordinator, which involves multiple administrative and educational tasks and, in some cases, teaching and research. The pitfalls of the role are described in order to highlight potential difficulties in incorporating change. The centrality of the role of the field education coordinator in effecting anti-oppression and antiracism in field education is described. Whiteness is examined to facilitate an understanding of imperialism, racism, dominance, privilege and oppression. In order to facilitate ongoing antiracist and anti-oppressive field education, the field education coordinator must begin with critical self reflections in order to fully understand how privilege and subordination are sustained. A space must be created in which all the constituents can dialogue and plan changes. Since the coordinator works closely with the student, faculty, agency and practitioner, there is rich opportunity and scope to incorporate an antiracist and anti-oppressive agenda. If the field education coordinator avoids this challenge, the field department will be unlikely to change. Social work as a profession is intricately linked to politics and political structures: dominance is embedded in its long political history. It is therefore critical to reflect on and examine the politics inherent in field education.

Chapter Three

The Politics of the Field

> Can social workers, while helping people deal with diverse social problems, act also as agents of fundamental social change, aimed at overcoming social injustice and oppression? (Gil 1998: 101)

Social services are located in the social welfare, health, education and employment sectors of the welfare state. These sites are always under scrutiny, if not outright attack. They are often in jeopardy because the operation of these programs are perceived by government and citizens to be a constant drain on the economy (Perera and Pugliese 1997, Kamerman 1996, Sink 1992). These socio-political realities impact heavily on social work teachings, research and practice. Socio-political issues are an integral part of the knowledge base of social work education, from the perspectives of policy analysis and bureaucratic organization to that of the individual client and community. According to Gray et al. (2000) "the political nature of social work derives from the activities in which social workers are engaged to remove social injustice" (1). Paying particular attention to human rights issues, social justice and inclusivity is at the heart of the philosophy of social work. However, there is a paradox in the profession: as agents of the state social workers must also confront personal, professional and institutional injustices, inequities and oppression. If a political vision is not incorporated to respond to systemic injustices, then we continue to maintain the dominant status quo of power, privilege and exploitation. Traditionally, radical social work was informed and produced through a political analysis of social ills. Radical social work practice has not been centralized within the profession. However it is increasingly evident that social workers must be involved in political processes, social action, policy analysis and human rights discourse. Transformative practice presupposes an understanding of global issues as they affect local practice. Grappling with the political dimension of social work is therefore critical for transformative change and liberatory practice.

This chapter examines how politics affect pedagogy, practice and student practica in social work field education. In the classroom there is dialogue, critique and understandings of the politics which underpin social services. In the practicum students witness the everyday exigencies of practice: if there is no space to incorporate a political analysis, then combating injustice and oppression becomes an idealistic vision rather than a dynamic inherent to their work. It is therefore critical to discuss how the field responds to political realities and, more importantly, how the student, field instructor and faculty can incorporate a political dialogue for practice.

Here I focus largely on the socio-political structures in Ontario to illustrate how a political agenda influences pedagogical and practice realities. Social work is greatly affected by political shifts, and agencies experience increased demands and restrictions due to funding constraints and fiscal crises which limit ability to provide adequate service to client and community. As workload increases, support diminishes, job insecurity emerges, workers become disillusioned and the field role becomes jeopardized. Many social workers assume the role of field instructors for students completing the practicum course. According to students, the practicum is the most critical course in the curriculum as it allows them to try out the theory gleaned in the classroom in practical ways at social service settings (Kadushin 1990). The placement agency plays a crucial role in offering the student the opportunity to practice skills while, at the same time, it receives the benefit of student labour (Wiebe 1996). The practicum offers students the opportunity to understand the fluidity of practice and to integrate the disparate micro and macro approaches. Field education must therefore be challenged to keep abreast of national and global trends which impact on social service delivery and on social work education (Donner 1996).

Over the years I have observed structural changes at agencies through my contacts with field instructors, other educational coordinators, faculty, students and through agency visits. As well, I became acutely aware of problematic work environments as students expressed their concerns at our integrative seminars and during faculty field visits. I concluded that it was necessary to critically analyze these socio-political changes which affect the role and responsibilities of field instructors as well as the ability of agencies to continue to provide and maintain excellent field placement learning opportunities for students. This chapter provides important information for educators and practitioners about the changing context of practice and the inherent difficulties presently facing the profession. In our profession this discussion is ongoing and can take different forms in response to shifting global, sociopolitical agendas. The recent protests at the World Summit in Quebec, regarding the Free Trade Agreement of the Americas, is a clear example of socio-political change arising from transnational agendas. It is important to understand that participation in movements for change does not only mean being physically present: people must work to ensure that the issues are understood, contested and included in the debates within organizations and universities. Often the connectedness of political decisions has to be illustrated so that students can situate the local within the global. As a result of trade agendas and transnational politics, agencies feel the burden of fiscal cuts, workers feel disenfranchised and oppressed (being asked to do more with less) and practicum students feel the anxieties and stresses of the workplace. According to Roche et al. (1999), there are four new trends which typify the present era and context for social work: the globalization of the world's capital, technology, trade and world markets; the rise of religious and political conservatism; the resurgence of ethnic nationalism and its notion of self-determination; and the dismantling of the welfare state (4). These areas affect the pedagogy and practice of social work and are inextricably tied to political agendas which are structurally inherent in universities, agencies and institutions. This analysis focuses on how politics informs field education, with particular emphasis on the planning, organization and integration of the practicum course with the rest of the curriculum. Although major parts of this chapter describe the socio-political realities relevant to one locality, it should be noted that threats and assaults to the welfare state are ongoing global concerns.

SOCIO-POLITICAL REALITIES

Social services have been deeply affected by the state's responses to globalization and transnational operations. An example of this shift has occurred over the past fifteen years in the province of Ontario, and also in other provinces across Canada, where there have been major assaults on the social service sector. The trends include downsizing and mergers or closures of hospitals, mental health programs and other social services. Many workers have also been laid off, as positions were eliminated and the institutions have restructured. Sometimes non-social work staff are employed to perform tasks formerly relegated to professionals. Many agencies and institutions respond to cutbacks by hiring managers qualified in business and administration to attract other sources of funding and to ensure that they stay "in the black." Such political battles for social services are central in most countries around the world (Midgley 1997, Mishra 1999). As the field education coordinator, I have observed the impacts of political whims on agencies and practitioners. These political changes affect the nature and process of pedagogy, practice and student learning. More significantly, the service users usually affected constitute the working class, the poor, visible minorities, those with disabilities, women and other marginalized groups with little socio-economic power.

These funding cuts to social services, health and education have resulted in strikes, massive layoffs, restructuring, downsizing, mergers and closures. The economic climate of uncertainty is cause for alarm: social service agencies have become sites of struggles. Clients feel the impact on a far greater scale because of reduced and insensitive service or, more disastrously, closure of critically needed services. The impact of these funding cuts has been monitored by various groups in order to organize action and to document the effect on people's lives. As well, agencies and organizations have worked together in coalitions to respond to ongoing government assaults on funding. These economic constraints have placed increased burdens and challenges on practitioners, who are being called upon to do more with less.

Since the Progressive Conservative party came to power in Ontario in 1995, the primary aim has been to fulfill a promise of a 30 percent income tax cut. In order to achieve this objective, numerous cuts to social services have occurred, and the term "slash and burn" has become a well-worn phrase. Social workers are affected in every sector, including schools, hospitals, ministries, community centres and immigrant and refugee service agencies. A survey of community-based social service agencies was conducted to examine the impact of cuts on social services. New user fees were introduced together with an increase in volunteer staff. These changes resulted in work displacement with deleterious effects on clients and workers (Social Planning Council 1996). In 1997 a report by the United Way of Greater Toronto indicated that the metro area was a community at risk due to recession, the results of which included rising poverty, a struggling economy and concerns about the capacity of social services to respond to social needs. Earlier information from The "Research Bulletin" edited by Metro Days of Action Research Department had already noted the cost of cuts to social services on clients. These included an increase in the use of the metropolitan area's food banks, a dramatic upswing in evictions, a 200 percent increase in waiting lists for child care and an increase in provision of shelter beds (Research Bulletin 1996). The Ontario Federation of Labour, in its report titled "The Common Sense Revolution: 449 Days of Destruction" (1996), examined areas such as education, social welfare, municipalities, housing and rent control, health and safety. All these areas reported massive cuts resulting in closures or a major reduction in services.

The Ontario Social Development Council (Costoglou 1996) summarized the cutbacks in Ontario and found the effects to be profound. Apart from documenting the cuts to various sectors and the impact on vulnerable populations, their report also puts forward an alternative economic perspective to counteract the rationale of the current government. They identify the way that social policy in Canada is being affected by profit-driven transnational corporations and influenced by right-wing think tanks (Costoglou 1996). The resulting focus on cuts to various helping services questions the government's priorities, which have focused on the creation of links with businesses to operate on a global scale. These reports highlight the shift towards transnational alliances and the need for business to penetrate the global market. In an effort to compete globally, the local economy and, more specifically, the social service sector become primary targets.

The most recent report, *Toronto at the Turning Point* by the United Way of Greater Toronto (1999), illustrates a "paradox" of an "improving economy and worsening social conditions" (1). Poverty, homelessness, lack of available and accessible housing, and increased use of food banks are some of the present social ills. Meanwhile the government is concentrating on reducing the budget and providing tax relief; these measures mainly benefit the wealthy. The increasing income gap between the rich and the poor is of concern since the polarization means that there will be less opportunity for individuals and families to achieve economic and social well-being. Recent global and transnational trends have created a diminished capacity on the part of the state to respond to social issues because of the perceived threats to the economy. The poor and disenfranchised are the primary targets of this global restructuring, since provision of social services is not a government priority. Just as there is an increased threat to the health, education and employment sectors, there is also the threat to professions such as social work, whose very essence lies in facilitating the improvement of the lives of those who are marginalized in society.

Immigration is a targeted area for government, which continues to increase the "head tax" for immigrants to enter the country. As these taxes rise there is an automatic decrease in particular populations, namely those from developing countries, who cannot afford the cost of immigrating. This tax is used to maintain the culture, colour and economic base of the dominant host countries. Affirmative action policies have been scrapped so that the white dominant group will continue to maintain centralized power. Black and Aboriginal people continue to be over-represented in the courts, and the penal system continues to wreak prejudicial and harsh judgements on them (Aylward 1999). According to a recent study, Toronto is rapidly becoming "segregated according to racial, ethnic, social and economic lines" (*Toronto Star* 2000). Huge inequalities exist in employment and education qualifications and opportunities, and poverty far exceeds the norm, especially for the Black population. These differences are substantively tied to race. Mothers on welfare are constantly being subjected to humiliating screening procedures. The latest incentive by the Ontario Government to have those on welfare cut off for life if any fraudulent behaviour is discovered is yet another assault on those who are oppressed. Surveillance tactics seriously affect the ability of social workers to intervene and facilitate a change process in clients' lives and also in the system, especially when they are themselves agents of control.

THE IMPACT OF CUTS ON CLIENTS

The Ontario Social Safety Network (1996) examined the impact of the 21.6 percent reduction in welfare allowances and found that these cuts affected the most vulnerable, namely children, single mothers, immigrants and people with disabilities. The City of York formed a group called York Agency Crisis Cutback Committee (YACCC) in the fall of 1995. They documented how people's lives were being affected as a result of the cutbacks. Some of their findings included: 78 percent of the 1332 respondents indicated being hurt by the cutbacks; 37 percent had lost jobs; over half indicated that their income was reduced; 37 percent reported being affected in the area of childcare; 43 percent affected by cuts to health; 34 percent were affected through the lack of community resources (YACCC 1996). All these results indicate the instability of health care, education and social services—key employment areas for social work graduates. The Ontario Social Development Council's Report (Costogbu 1996) described the various cutbacks to about fifty agencies and over twenty communities across Ontario. The report summarized the effect on vulnerable populations and introduced alternative economic perspectives to counteract the present government's rationale.

A more recent study by the United Way of Greater Toronto (1999) indicates that the recession of the early 1990s affected the city more than the surrounding areas. Poverty has worsened—female-led single parents are among the poorest people in Toronto. Stricter eligibility criteria mean that many cannot qualify for government income support, and affordable housing is limited. The ghettoizing of poor families translates into negative futures. Given such a grim economic situation, which includes job instability and ongoing threats of further cutbacks, social service agencies continue to be in crisis. Services to clients have been reduced and continue to be in jeopardy. The profession of social work is being challenged to operate differently, and social work students and educators need to understand these implications.

THE CHANGING NATURE OF PRACTICE

Given the above realities it is imperative to pay attention to the current climate at social service agencies to determine the impact on field education. This analysis integrates a variety of perspectives including a small survey, political reports, observations and discussions with students, faculty and field instructors. The survey provides feedback from practicum students and field instructors in 1996, when the first round of funding cuts were being implemented. These cuts have not decreased, although currently both the federal and provincial governments boast huge budget surpluses, while homelessness and poverty are on the rise.

This study utilized surveys which were sent to approximately fifty agencies in the metropolitan Toronto area where students were fulfilling the practicum course. The survey consisted of open-ended questions relating to the impact of funding cuts, restructuring and downsizing on human service agencies. Both student and agency participant were asked to elaborate on their observation of the role of the student in the practicum, in light of the changing context of practice brought about by the devolution of social services and the deployment and dismissal of workers. The survey was accompanied by a letter of introduction outlining the rationale for the study, ensuring confidentiality and offering feedback if desired. The field instruction seminars at the school and faculty visits to the agencies were sites for further discussions, as social work practitioners discussed the work climate and the effects on practice. Some of the questionnaires were completed at these seminars as field instructors were able to elaborate on their struggles within the workplace.

FINDINGS: THE AGENCIES

Out of the fifty agencies surveyed, thirty (60 percent) completed and returned the questionnaire. Twenty-five of these agencies were from the Metro area while five others were from outlying communities. The highest number of responses came from agencies serving families and children. The major source of funding for twenty-four (80 percent) of these agencies came from the provincial government, while twenty-three (77 percent) reported that their agencies had experienced direct funding cuts from the provincial government. One agency that did not report provincial cuts indicated that they were in danger of being privatized. Some agencies with external sources of funding reported that they also had to make cuts to services. Two other agencies did not report budget cuts—one was privately funded and the other functioned almost entirely with volunteers and one staff position.

Respondents were asked to indicate the number of employees and the number of layoffs which resulted from funding cuts. Thirty layoffs were reported, with ten of these occurring at smaller agencies (one to ten staff). Thirteen agencies reported that these cuts would affect their capacity to take students. Sixteen agencies also described changes which needed to occur either with regards to social work education or the nature of the particular student, if placements were to continue. Agencies were requesting that students be flexible, mature, experienced self-starters. There was also an urgency for the university to prepare students for the realities of practice involved in relating to organizational structures and bureaucracies, and in advocacy, policy and social action.

The students
Nineteen students (38 percent) out of a total of fifty completed the questionnaire. The lower response rate was due in part to students not receiving the questionnaire sent to their respective placement sites. Fourteen of the nineteen (74 percent) students reported that their placement agencies have had to make cuts either to service or staff. Eight students (42 percent) reported that the cuts affected their basic practicum education (strike at agency) as well as their personal sense of well-being (tension, uncertainty). A total of thirteen (68 percent) felt increased pressure in the placement due to government cuts. All the respondents indicated that their practicum experience had increased their knowledge about the political climate and its impact on social services agencies. The most severe effects of budget cuts were felt by the three students who believed that

their placements were in jeopardy of early termination due to continued cuts to service.

Four students (21 percent) indicated that they had adopted social action positions against the cuts in their practicum setting, by assisting with media response bulletins and supporting workers on strike. Four students (21 percent) indicated that budget cuts affected supervision time with their field instructors and eleven (58 percent) reported that they discussed these concerns with their faculty advisors. Thirteen students (68 percent) indicated that they had discussed issues about funding cuts at their integrative seminars with their faculty advisor and a group of students.

There has been a notable shift upward in the requests from field instructors for more mature and experienced students. There is also a demand for flexibility and a readiness to assume a caseload with immediate job responsibilities. There is a de-emphasis on teaching and learning, decreasing availability of placement sites and less time for supervision. Field instructors are partnering around the supervision role—while this approach has benefits and merit, sometimes the resulting lack of clarity of roles can be damaging for the student. Many practitioners, especially within child welfare agencies and hospitals, face the demands arising from decentralization of services, restructuring, mergers and downsizing. Workload is increasing, caseloads are burgeoning and threats of malpractice in areas of child welfare have resulted in the creation of competency modules and reduced participation of workers in field instruction. Kolar et al. (2000) state that field instructors reported that the managed care approach caused them to reduce the time spent with students and also to change the criteria for selecting a student. Competency-based guidelines have also increased surveillance in the workplace and severely restricted political and critical forms of practice (Rossiter 2000).

At the same time, universities are also struggling with cutbacks and increases in class size, which decrease the opportunities for shared interaction and skill-based learning. Field education programs are also affected by these university pressures and constraints (Jarman-Rhode et al. 1997). All of these developments, together with insufficient field administrative support, impact heavily on the practicum. As we are being coerced into increasing our numbers we are also aware that the pool of applicants has dwindled and choices are fewer. The student body tends to be younger and more inexperienced. Students also need to augment income through employment and have many other responsibilities which affect their commitment to the practicum. There is also a high turnover of field instructors because of the greater job demands; many times we are compelled to use less experienced field instructors. Field coordinators also spend more time troubleshooting, developing new placements and monitoring and responding to everyday issues. There is little time for research and dissemination of information to students, faculty and field instructors.

In a recent study, Jarman-Rhode et al. (1997) examined the changing context of social work practice through an analysis of how political and economic developments have reshaped traditional social work practice. Funding cuts, privatization and cost containment in the human service field cause dramatic swings in access and availability of services. They focus their discussion on the learning environment for the student and do an overall examination of current social work education and practice. Their recommendations include promoting the value and centrality of social work, collaborating with the community on research projects and developing outcome measures, professional leadership, activism, political action and licensing (34–37). Selber et al. (1998) echo these sentiments and add that field education is the capable location to bridge the university and practice communities through innovative programs and research partnerships.

DISCUSSION

The discussion will focus on three themes which emerge from the survey findings, from discussions with field instructors and faculty field advisors and from the socio-political climate. These areas illustrate present difficulties in the profession and signal the critical importance of maintaining a political vision. The themes are workplace culture/stress, the dilemmas facing students and the changing context for practice. Implications for students, social work field education, educators and practitioners will be addressed.

WORKPLACE STRESS/CULTURE

The primary role of social workers is to facilitate the improvement of people's life situations through a range of direct and indirect services. Social workers have always struggled to maintain this objective amid cutbacks and fiscal restraints. Bracken and Wamsley (1992) describe the evolution of the welfare state and the implications for continuing education for social workers.

> The ideological and fiscal changes occurring to the welfare state suggest major implications for social work practice. A reduction in resources available for social work services places demands on social workers to provide "more with less." (23)

As workers continue to struggle under economic constraints they are seldom given opportunities to discuss political realities. Social workers also feel very vulnerable in their jobs and therefore become overly cautious in their behaviours and attitudes. Many agencies do not provide the space to dialogue about changes and, as a result, workers also fail to engage students in such discussion. Yet, social workers construct relationships with clients for empowerment and change. Students observe such role contradictions among workers and within the organizational bureaucracies. The buzzwords "more with less," "restructuring" and "downsizing" cause alarm and feelings of vulnerability. As jobs are being cut and more tasks are being added to already high workloads, workers feel a sense of powerlessness not unlike their clients. The conundrum which occurs is not accorded sufficient attention because of restraints and methods of surveillance in the workplace (Rossiter, Prilletinsky and Bowers 1996).

Students reported tension, uncertainty and anxiety due to layoffs and increased workloads. One student at a health care setting, for example, reported "anxiety about layoffs throughout the Social Work Department—particularly noticeable with practicum supervisor." Two other student placements were interrupted because the workers went on strike; the students stated that the workers were "pushed to their limits and often required student and volunteer help." Three students placed at different school boards described long waiting lists for service. As referral and outreach services from agencies such as Children's Aid were drastically reduced, one student felt greater pressure to provide more effective and efficient services. Another student reported that because there was a lack of available referral agencies for school boards, the caseloads for school social workers remained high, resulting in increased stress and tension at the board office. At one government ministry, student practica were also interrupted because of a strike; future planning was difficult because of fears of closure. One student stated that "employee morale affects service delivery. Agency focus is to be more task-oriented to heighten efficiency with fewer resources. The consumer is not as important as once was or should be." Supervision became informal and limited because of time constraints. Supervisors have reported that they have a strict, inflexible time allotment to attend meetings and seminars. Their angst over these situations is apparent. One faculty colleague reported that, during the break at a seminar which she was facilitating at a social work setting, everyone rushed to check phone messages. This indicated to her a workplace culture of stress. Time for reflection and discussions about workplace culture is seemingly non-existent.

The ethno-specific agencies reported significant cutbacks and closure of services. One student, who reported feeling pressured into completing a large volume of work, stated that staff morale was admittedly low because of job uncertainty. Another student felt that this uncertainty and the general lack of morale contributed to communication problems between students and supervisors. It is clear that the impact of the cuts is being felt deeply among workers and students and within institutions. There is a ripple effect which occurs at settings such as the school board when their referral agencies decrease support because of cutbacks and shrinking resources.

Field instructors were not asked direct questions related to the impact of the cuts on the agency or whether there was tension in the agency surrounding these changes. Instead the survey focus was on the availability of and protocol for practicum sites for students in the context of the cuts to services. Fifty-five percent of the field instructors did not think that funding cuts would affect their decision to take students in placement. Student placement was viewed as a mutually beneficial experience, with students identified as an asset to the program. Supervisors mentioned their own commitment to teaching. This feedback mirrors the findings of Bocage et al. (1995) where, despite the cutbacks and changes, agencies reported a commitment to student training reflected in experimenting with different forms of supervision. Unfortunately in a climate of restraint there is minimal time to research and implement innovative supervisory approaches. Nine agencies reported that further layoffs may jeopardize future student placements. Others believed that, since their positions were vulnerable, so were student placements.

One instructor indicated that there was a "danger" in using students as staff. Three instructors noted that they are even more committed to student placement with the cuts to staff, although the reasons behind such commitment remain unclear. The ethno-specific agencies indicated the need for students to have more initiative and independent work habits. As workload increased, there was also less time for student supervision. One counselling agency indicated that "we are even more concerned to make productive use of students to deliver core services." Another agency indicated that they needed the fee-for-service revenue which is reduced when there are "student counsellors." These views about student placement cause some concern with respect to the education role of the field instructor and agency. The comments reflect the ongoing dilemmas about restructuring and downsizing which should be taken seriously by educators and practitioners.

DILEMMAS FACING STUDENTS

Factors affecting student satisfaction in placement relate to the quality of field instruction, desirability for inclusion at the agency and explanations by the field instructor (Fortune and Abramson 1993). One student indicated that the placement students (including students from other universities) were excluded from staff meetings. They felt that they had to be grateful to be there on placement; some even felt pushed to leave. On a personal skill level students felt they needed to be "more versatile, adaptable, [and] have survival skills and power" in order to fit into the agency culture. The following are combined responses from students who felt that they had gained valuable knowledge and awareness of "the impact of social and economic factors and the coping abilities of families; the political reality of mergers; the relationship between government and public service agency; learning to work under budgetary constraints and how politics both influence and are influenced by economic conditions." Students also recognized how employee morale affects service delivery and many discussed their fears about their future and the profession itself. Graduate school appeared to be a first option for these B.S.W. students. Although students felt that they had gained knowledge and experience in new areas, the tension and stress level appeared to impinge upon their ability to fully participate in the agency. A key question at this point is this: How can we theorize and build knowledge and skills which mirror current sociopolitical realities?

Discussions with students at integrative seminars and at the agency revealed that there is a climate of uncertainty with regard to the status of student placements in several agencies. Some agencies, which formerly accepted B.S.W. students, are now only offering placements for M.S.W. students, and, even then, they require mature, experienced and flexible students. Learning is less emphasized in this scenario where the expectations to perform indicate less need to supervise, dialogue and engage in teaching and learning. There is also the acceptance of "cheap labour," which is in direct conflict with the educational aspect of field education (Wiebe 1996). There are growing concerns about liability, safety and highly complex and diverse client issues. Many students also enter social work with their own history of social problems which surface quite acutely in the practicum (see Chapter Seven.)

THE CHANGING CONTEXT FOR PRACTICE

Despite precarious conditions at social service institutions, many field instructors, some of whom also shared that their jobs were in jeopardy, reported that students continue to be welcomed at the agency. At pre-screening interviews students are being warned that acceptance decisions may change with further restructuring and/or their own employment status at the agency. One student who was successfully interviewed was subsequently informed that the agency had to deny him the placement because of restructuring. The same student had another successful interview but on the first day of practicum an uproar erupted because the manager realized that they had admitted too many practicum students into a workplace rife with tension and conflict. The field instructor called to say that the student had to leave, but, through tense negotiations, the student was permitted to stay. Studies indicate that practitioners take students because of a sense of professional duty, a desire to teach, a sense of accomplishment, the desire to influence another's professional development and to keep up with the latest knowledge (Bell and Webb 1992). These findings certainly concur with results from this study. However, it is important to consider how these motivating factors are affected under the present work conditions. The survey results suggest that field instructors continue to value students in spite of the funding cuts and restraints. The recent demands for more experienced students, however, could denote a climate where the emphasis may be shifting to a focus on agency gain rather than on a reciprocal teaching and learning process. The students described tenuous work environments, workplace tension, stress and anxiety.

Studies also indicate that the supervisory relationship is a crucial factor associated with student satisfaction in placement (Yeung and Tsor-Kui 1996). Adequate emotional support, ability to observe the field instructor, and the facilitating of creative understandings of theory and practice are also important for placement satisfaction. In this survey a number of students reported tension and insisted that the current economic climate affected their practicum experience. One field instructor stated that there was a danger that the student would be viewed as staff while others are demanding that students be innovative, independent and flexible enough to function with minimal supervision. There is a cost to education and learning for the student when there is limited opportunity to engage with the field instructor in order to learn and be challenged.

In this time of budgetary constraints, how can we guarantee quality supervision and a supportive learning environment? Other questions of paramount importance emerge: Is the field education model adequate in providing meaningful learning for social work students? What strategies are needed to address the current environment? How can student learning be maximized and how can the school provide support for field instructors and agencies with the community? How can the practicum department provide multicultural sites for learning when these agencies continue to be jeopardized by the current socio-political climate? Moreover, how can students begin to respond to these political issues in their placement without feeling marginalized? Recognizing the changes occurring and the action being taken are critical in order to readjust and restructure in an attempt to continue to serve those who have been disenfranchised in society. The next section attempts to respond to these questions.

IMPLICATIONS FOR THE PRACTICUM AND SOCIAL WORK EDUCATION

Rossiter, Prilletinsky and Bowers (1996) conducted a study of "workers' lived experience of ethics, workers' conception of ethics, and workers' understanding of obstacles to ethics" (46). While ethics per se is not the focus of this chapter, their findings relating to workplace culture and organizational structure have direct implications for understanding workers' abilities to function in a climate of uncertainty. Students reported tension, uncertainty and low morale among workers. It appears that workers have little opportunity to discuss their feelings because of increased workload and job instability and vulnerability. Rossiter et al. (1996) suggest that in the current political economic climate marked by cutbacks and downsizing, workers feel at risk to discuss concerns. They note that

> this broad political threat has produced a rigid definition of professionalism—to be credible, correct, certain…. Workers risk feeling and being seen as unprofessional if they seek a safe place for ambivalent and uncertain ethical dialogue…. A contradiction exists when the people with little power must risk seeming unprofessional to those with more power…. Workers often feel frustrated. (46)

Organizational strictures, bureaucratic processes and hierarchical systems can deleteriously affect the work environment. If workers are unable to discuss political issues, workplace stress and ethical dilemmas, their struggles will most likely be felt by clients and students. Educators need to address these concerns and allow for critical inquiry and understandings of how power is produced and operates within organizations. Workplace struggles are rooted within the current political climate. When there are charges of negligence made against one worker in an agency, the whole system is affected. The system responds by becoming more guarded and controlled. Surveillance tactics, which especially target front line workers, are deployed. These constraints also affect the ability of workers to engage in political debate since they are focused on managing their work. Being considered "political" signifies being marked as volatile and confrontational. Students learn to read these cues early on in the agency and can feel stifled and reluctant to speak, disregard a political agenda or challenge the system, at times to their peril.

Cooper (1996) states that increasing constraints within agencies demand that the field work in an "overtly reciprocal nature," with more support for the agency from the university. The schools may need to play a more active role and offer more concrete support to agencies through collaboration about projects and continuing education. The field instructor also needs to learn ways to facilitate understanding of the political contexts within which students' actions take place and the political consequences. Workers demonstrate these political understandings in the manner in which they themselves respond to the political dimensions of their work. Often students report dissonance within an organization because of impending layoffs, funding cuts and issues about oppression, racism and marginalization. Students are hesitant to initiate discussion with their supervisor because of their vulnerable position, which involves being evaluated by the supervisor and needing references to secure future employment. It is therefore critical that the field instructor provides the space and facilitates discussions about the political implications of practice. For example, it is not ideal anymore to adopt a psychodynamic approach without also critically analyzing the liberal perspective that the individual agency is the principal locus for achieving positive change. The structural forces of oppression resulting in funding cuts to social programs need to be viewed and discussed in a political context, in order to assist in helpful change responses. The university also has to be attuned to the changes occurring within agencies and seek innovative ways to be supportive if it wishes to sustain excellent learning sites.

Deeper analysis is required within the curriculum of field education to situate the current trends in practice. Midgley and Livermore (1996) suggest that schools, in collaboration with the community, develop effective community outreach and translate theory into professional practice situations. Field education can provide collaborative learning opportunities through faculty field research projects which would entail group field work options. Some instructors indicated the need for students to be more trained in crisis intervention, management and organizational skills. Consideration should be given to how classroom teaching can correlate with the skills needed for effective social work practice. In the research reported earlier, all the students found that, given the current situation, they had gained knowledge and still benefited tremendously from the practicum in terms of survival skills, advocacy and social action—skills not easily grasped in the classroom. Field instructors should be encouraged to visit classrooms so that more of the practical aspects can be linked to the theory.

It is important to note that the quality of field instruction depends heavily on the availability of time for planning and supervising, space for students to conduct the work and level of knowledge of social work theories and practice (Donner 1996). It is imperative that resources shift to support students, agencies and field instructors in terms of seminars, workshops, visits and liaison opportunities so the learning continues to be meaningful. It is also critical that the field education department seeks creative ways to support the field instructors. Some areas could include free workshops and seminars at the school, electronic mail accounts and Internet access, and library privileges. Many agencies can no longer afford professional development training, and the school and individual faculty can assist agencies with continuing education initiatives and training. The school must be proactive in its provision of information and education in accordance with the needs of the field instructors. Letters can be sent to supervisors and directors of agencies giving recognition to the role of the field instructor, and continuing education credits to attend training sessions are further incentives. Efforts to link with the community should remain fluid in order to coincide with ongoing structural changes.

The curriculum in social work must include a detailed analysis of the political dilemmas of the practice of social work. According to Gil (1998), social workers

> require an attitude of experimentation and critical consciousness toward their practice, and they need to help one another to evaluate it, and to deal constructively with resistance from admin-

istrators, supervisors, and colleagues in organizations practising along conventional lines. (101)

Gil (1998) promotes "support-and-study groups" for radical social workers to confront injustice and oppression through practice. Critical intellectual, experiential and practical approaches to maintaining a political vision are necessary for social work to attain its stated goals and objectives. Educators teach within traditionally oppressive structures and can also feel the "paradox" of trying to unsettle hegemonic discourse. Classroom and field placement agencies need to provide "liberated spaces" for intellectual and political discussion. These spaces will minimize tensions, conflicts and dilemmas which political responses engender. If such structures are entrenched in education, and field instructors and agencies are informed and educated simultaneously, then students will be more inclined to incorporate a political analysis in which to confront injustice and oppression. The school needs to include a political perspective in all aspects of social work education. Not only should students be taught about the political economy and issues, but critical political practice debates should be encouraged to facilitate and incorporate such thinking into their practice. The practicum is an ideal site to encourage such interrogations, provided that the skills and substantive political knowledge of issues are part of their preparation and training. In order to adequately include a political context for practice and ways to incorporate "intersubjective approaches" for sustainable supports in the work environment, there needs to be non-threatening spaces to dialogue and differ.

CONCLUSION

The political transformation of the last decade has impacted heavily on social services. There have been cutbacks, reallocation of funds, downsizing, restructuring, privatization, mergers and closures of agencies and institutions which provided services for those who are disenfranchised in the community. The swiftness and severity of funding cuts to social services, health and education have serious implications for social work education and practice. These political realities create critical dimensions and dynamics for social work education and practice. The new transnational age has especially played a large role as local governments respond to their perceived powerlessness by cutting critical services and introducing devastating surveillance mechanisms on their clients.

Field instructors, students and educators need to confront the challenges posed by the current environment of restructuring, downsizing and deployment. Increased awareness of the impact of funding cuts and of the ways in which educators, practitioners and students can create a sustained political vision is needed in order to legitimize the profession. As has been noted, the field education component of the practicum is seriously affected by any political changes to social services. New opportunities for critical thinking and debate over these issues should be encouraged and facilitated between schools and the community. Social work needs to be promoted in the community and in the political arena through collaborative research projects and political action. The need to respond in innovative ways is essential to maintain standards of practice and pedagogical approaches with emphasis on ways to enhance and maintain excellence in field education. Innovative placements can be further developed, and new and improved ways of instruction can be implemented in order to minimize the burdens created by job instability and downsizing. It is apparent that we have to begin to challenge ourselves to understand workplace struggles and to be continuously adept at incorporating changes to fit the current demands on service. These economic concerns and socio-political challenges reflect global reality and the need to recognize practice in an interdependent context.

Ethno-specific agencies have received major cutbacks as have services for seniors, children and persons with disabilities. We need to pay attention to these trends and continue to monitor changes and organize action to respond to these injustices. We ought to explore alternative ways to supervise students if an experienced pool of field instructors is disappearing. The school needs to be supportive and creative in their role and function with the agency. The discussion of the role of the agency in field education helps to ground the political context of field education. Clearly, political behaviours continue to mark everyone's lives. Creating liberated spaces for political dialogue is a beginning.

Chapter Four

The Agency Context

Human service agencies offer an array of programs which employ social workers with graduate and undergraduate degrees. Agencies are also the training sites for social work students; they act as the medium for the successful fulfillment of the practicum course. An excellent placement site encourages and facilitates critical, reflexive and transformative approaches to learning and practice. The agency, however, has not been under scrutiny to determine organizational factors which may impinge on its ability to facilitate this critical course. Agencies should be evaluated to ensure that they can, in fact, deliver such placements. Giddings, Thompson and Holland (1997) state that evaluation of agencies has been "anecdotal, intuitive and dependent on the source" (26). Since, in this current climate of downsizing, restructuring and job insecurities, the agency is enmeshed in political battles, especially to secure funding, it can be a contentious site for the student. As we discuss structural inequalities and oppression in this text, the agency is central to this theme, situated as it is, within the broader contextual framework of the practicum. The organization is a critical area to examine because it offers training opportunities for social work students in the graduate and undergraduate programs.

This chapter critically explores how the various locations where students complete the practicum can be inclusive of diverse realities. It is necessary to have an integrated change process in all levels of the practicum, if effective and ongoing change is to occur. As noted in earlier chapters, there are several constraints placed on agencies and workers which can have adverse effects on the placement. When students arrive at the agency with hopes of gaining critical perspectives, and these are unmet, disillusionment can ensue. Students may be hesitant to challenge the agency for fear of unsettling relations. The university and agency differ in their expectations of students and their philosophies about learning and practice. These differences can evoke tensions and anxieties. It is also incumbent on the agency to promote antidiscriminatory and transformative practice. Here I describe the agency's role in ensuring adherence to antiracist and anti-oppressive principles. Change efforts will be highlighted together with some challenges for the university administration to undertake in order to ensure inclusivity at practicum locations. As public institutions subject to government regulations, the university and the agency suffer the deleterious effects of global politics and neo-liberal agendas. Because they reflect the state's agenda, organizations, therefore, can be viewed as oppressive sites.

INSTITUTIONAL RACISM AND OPPRESSION

Racism is a palpable dynamic within institutions and organizations. Social service agencies are no exception to this ongoing disturbing phenomenon. According to Fleras and Elliott (1999),

> *Institutional racism* refers to the process by which organizational practices and procedures are used either deliberately or inadvertently to discriminate against "others." By institutional racism, we are not simply referring to individual acts of racism within the confines of an institution or workplace. Rather, we are referring to the rules, procedures, rewards, and practices that have the intent (systematic) or effect (systemic) of excluding or denying some because of who they are, how they live, and what they do. (81–82)

Racism and oppression are embedded within social service agencies. Although the mandate of the social service agency is to help those who are disenfranchised in society, hierarchical power and privileged positions influence workplace politics. These contradictions hound the profession in many ways and create dissonance within those workers who strive to balance dual spaces. Ferguson (1996) states that one of the most obvious signs of dominance is the absence of people of colour in management positions (37). Many students report that the agency serves a very diverse group, yet the workers are predominantly or exclusively white. Likewise students who have come out as gay, lesbian or bisexual strive to locate an agency where they will not have to submerge their sexual identity or face homophobia. Students with disabilities have enormous struggles to "get in the door" both physically and psychologically. They are refused interviews because the agency believes they cannot accommodate the disability (see Chapter Nine). These omissions in policy are covert acts of institutional racism and oppression.

Fleras and Elliott (1999) refer to institutional inclusiveness to define a process of proactive work toward dismantling barriers and engaging diversity both internally and externally (329). Issues relating to hierarchical power and inequality need to be fully examined and explored. The agency needs to have clear policies and procedures to respond to harassment and chilly climate issues and mechanisms in place to ensure that services are culturally sensitive and appropriate. Sensitivity training and cross-cultural understandings have become the mantra to assist institutions and workers to respond to a racist and oppressive society. However, limiting the discussion to culture and ethnic variety does not allow for questioning power, privilege and the preservation of hegemony in Whiteness and "White Nationalism."[1] (Bonilla-Silva 2000: 202). Also, sensitivity training sessions are organized to respond to particular dynamics relating to culture and ethnicity. Instead, training ought to be ongoing since it is necessary to constantly theorize and gain new insights into how political shifts and global trends help to secure dominance. Lloyd (1998) argues that training focuses on the individual as the agent of change, who then depends on managerial monitoring rather than her/his own ability to focus on political struggles.

Ferguson (1996) outlines some issues which would assist in the making of an antiracist and anti-oppressive organization. These relate to how the agency models antiracist and anti-oppressive values, through equitable opportunities for minority members, encouraging competency and sensitivity in workers, providing conceptual knowledge of race, ethnicity, power and efficacy in helping, and through its responses to community change (36). The staff at all levels of the organization must be cognizant of systemic, institutional and individual forms of discrimination. Representation is a key to embracing and promoting equality. The agency ought to reflect the general demographics of the population: if there are clusters of particular populations in its locality, stronger efforts must be made to employ members from that particular group. Likewise the workplace should be physically accessible, and the environment ought to promote and reflect an acceptance of all people. When members of minority groups are hired into a white majority space, there should be support systems in place to help retain them; otherwise, there will be exclusion through systemic racist and oppressive practices (Wilson 1997).

POLICIES AND PROCEDURES

Rogers (1996) describes the efforts in the U.K. to incorporate antidiscrimination guidelines in field teaching. These efforts were met with resistance and much debate because practice teachers questioned the competence and knowledge base of those designated to teach in these areas. Tensions also arose because of the belief that introducing a dialogue on oppression encourages a hierarchy based on whose oppression is greater. It is clear that, if the agency does not demonstrate a commitment to inclusive student learning, the issues get derailed into a political agenda relating to hierarchy. In major metropolitan areas where there is competition for student placements, this commitment may not be clearly delineated or easily fulfilled. Not all schools have insisted that agencies provide student training as part of their overall goals and objectives. Student training is therefore viewed as an appendage, separate to the overall functioning of the agency. Since field coordinators are under constant pressure to find new placements, they may resort to sending students to agencies without fully researching the setting. They are constantly responding to budgetary constraints—managing and creating new programs and increasing admission with overall insufficient resources. Efforts to connect issues of diversity and antiracism to an oppressive structure can cause tensions, hostility and havoc. It is critical in an organized change process to consider and provide for process, dialogue and supportive management structures.

AGENCY AND UNIVERSITY: TENSIONS AND CONFLICTS

Field education depends on the link between agency and university. The agency and university consist of two subcultures operating simultaneously to delineate the exigencies of pedagogy and practice. The university is usually set apart from the dynamics of practice: academic teaching often lacks analyses of the practice dilemmas which social workers face on a daily basis. Witkin (1998) describes conflicts which may occur between the agency and university. Field instructors complain about the irrelevance of the academic curricula and research to the daily issues they face in their work, and academics undervalue "clinical" practice, standardized assessments and competency requirements in practice. Although the agencies and academic institutions are involved in the training of students, process and task expectations can differ. The goal of the school is to facilitate students' critical thinking skills in practice while the agency demands that students have practice skills and knowledge about community resources.

Witkin (1998) states that tensions can also arise because of difference of status. Academic knowledge is viewed as more superior than practical knowledge: the professor can more easily become a highly valued part of the agency than a practitioner can integrate into an academic environment (390). Sheldon (1978) suggests that there are two subcultures which operate between the agency and university—a theoretical subculture in academia and an anti-intellectual subculture which is rooted in practice. Human service agencies want social workers to meet agency needs as defined by the agency and not as prescribed by the school. At our field instructor seminars some of these tensions are evident. One particular instructor commented that he came to the seminar on poverty to hear the position of our school on the topic. Students are taught the political dimension of poverty by analyzing the structural forces of oppression, which include political mandates, economic realities and overall relegation of resources. When students are placed in settings such as child welfare and begin to introduce an analysis of the structural forces of inequity, tensions can arise.

Although some of these tensions are inevitable given the differences in structure and role, there are ways in which the agency and university can complement each other to challenge inequities and confront oppression. The university depends on the agency to provide grist for academic inquiry. As a professional school we need to be informed about cutting-edge practice and also about the structures and socio-political and economic changes affecting agencies. We cannot afford to educate students to operate only from a political perspective without also teaching applicable and practical skills to effect a political approach. Universities need to validate different kinds of knowledge and must recognize the skills and experience of the practitioners. If the agencies are not valued, even while being critiqued, then opportunities for change and redress will be limited. Systemic inequalities can abound when tensions and conflict are overlooked. Students have to be able to negotiate differences as they are located among staff, organizational procedures, clientele and expectations of work.

AGENCY PERSONNEL

Many agencies have educational coordinators who maintain direct links about placements with the school. It is essential for these coordinators to understand school curricula in order to speak to the social workers on staff about the field program. It is then incumbent on this coordinator to be aware of anti-oppression guidelines and know how to seek training for the staff to adopt this critical teaching and learning role. The coordinator needs to ensure that the agency is aware of the school's philosophy and of the diversity of student body. Where there are no educational coordinators, there should be a concerted effort by the school to produce material for the agency to read prior to accepting students. In some areas where there is little competition for field placements this task can be readily accomplished. However, in urban areas, where there are three or more universities and colleges, the goal of instituting anti-oppression policies becomes more challenging, though still achievable. If possible there should be meetings with potential agencies prior to engagement with the practicum. Since in large metropolitan areas it is almost impossible to visit every site to ensure that there is an understanding of the program, we need to rely on letters, our manuals, phone calls, electronic mail, seminars, evaluations and field fairs to promote the school's approach.

RECOGNITION AND COMPENSATION

Field instructors act as the principal course directors for the practicum. They expend considerable energy preparing and orienting the student to the agency, teaching practice skills and facilitating the integration of theory and practice, as well as assisting students in enhancing professional identity. Often field instructing is added onto an already heavy case load (see Chapter Five). However, the feedback from these field instructors is that their instruction is not valued at the agency and that there is no organizational compensation or benefit for being a continuing professional educator. Some agencies have an organized approach to taking students, in which they provide seminar and orientation activities as well as staff recognition luncheons. This process also benefits the students. However, the agencies do not shift the worker's load to accommodate the time and demands of field teaching. The practitioner who requests a practicum student is usually committed to the profession and wants to remain on the cutting edge of theory and practice. Some workplaces do have a mandate for field placements, but workers still have to volunteer, and there is usually minimal, if any, concessions to their workload. Also many field instructors do not have time to attend training seminars at the school. These are critical issues for agencies to discuss and recognize in their commitment to sustaining our profession.

As many schools vie for placement agencies it is also necessary for the agency to develop an equitable approach to linking and dealing with field educational coordinators from various schools. While some agencies may have a history with a particular university, it is important that there be equitable procedures to allow for similar opportunities for all social work students. The mutual benefits of placements should be clearly outlined and understood, so the approach is not only one of gaining student labour (Wiebe 1996) but also one of teaching and providing a space for dialogue and learning. Recognition and appreciation of the field instructor should also be included in the field education package.

REDRESSING CURRENT INEQUALITIES

The overall structure, management, philosophy and culture of the agency are critical to effect useful ongoing analyses of race and oppression. In summary, some guidelines are as follows:

- A mandate and document that explicitly outline the process for recruiting students should be prepared.
- This document/manual should include policies which discuss how racism, classism, homophobia and other injustices are taken up within the agency.
- The document should be updated regularly and be the orientation manual for students.
- The agency should be open to engaging in critical dialogue about the political nature of practice.
- The agency should be knowledgeable about the university mission statement, philosophy and curricula.
- The agency should have available and updated copies of the field manual which must be read by those involved with students.
- Likewise the agency should provide the school with program materials outlining their mission statement, philosophy, programs, mandate and community resources.
- The agency must ensure that there is an orientation and adaptation period at the beginning of the placement.

- The agency should seek to reduce the workload of the field instructor to engage in teaching and learning.
- The agency must allow time for field instructors to attend training seminars at the university and other relevant professional training.
- The educational coordinator at the agency must maintain links with the school and also understand the forces of oppression.
- The agency should demand that the school faculty visit the agency to discuss issues relating to the practicum.
- The agency must engage in ongoing debates about the political nature of practice, understanding how racism and oppression are understood and maintained.
- These policies and debates must also be communicated to board members, administrative staff and workers.

CONCLUSION

The agency is the conduit for the practicum. It is the site of practicum learning, and it affords students the opportunity to hone their skills and assess their professional suitability. The agency offers the space for students to test the theory gleaned in the classroom in a setting which promotes and values the importance of critical practice. In order to ensure these goals, the board and staff need to accept and incorporate the guidelines and expectations of the school. The university must also value and promote these sites for learning and ensure that the agency is knowledgeable about the school curriculum, philosophy and mission. The politics of the agency also influence the work climate for field instructors and these issues should be included in their supervisory discussions. For example, if there are cutbacks and field instructors are especially vulnerable, these issues can be sensitively shared with the students. Often the students feel the tensions and are hesitant to broach the subject for fear of reprisal.

There can also be tensions between the university and the agency about academic practice concerns, and these effects can be keenly felt in placement. Students engaged in political activity and social advocacy may have the tendency to push the boundaries at agencies where there is an entrenched hierarchy and overt systemic inequalities. These politically motivated students need to grapple with the skills necessary to engage in a discussion about systemic change. Likewise the agency needs to understand the school's curriculum and discuss a theoretical as well as a political understanding of practice in a global context. It is through these educational experiences that awareness and advocacy for change will ensue. The field instructor, as a participant in the agency, can act as a critical guide in this field teaching process. It is important therefore to analyze this role to ensure equitable professional practice.

NOTE

1. White nationalism indicates that through liberal discourse of culture, ethnic variety and in accounts of difference, Whiteness maintains a dominance and privileged location. This discourse allows Whites in the West to defend their racial privilege without appearing to be "racist."

Chapter Five

Power Dynamics, Knowledge Production and Social Location: The Role of the Field Instructor

> The responsiveness and responsibilities of our field have been greatly enhanced by the development of differentiated knowledge. (Chambon and Irving 1998: xv)

The field instructors are the treasured resources of the practicum. Schools of social work are continuously building relationships with social service agencies and institutions to recruit expert field teachers to supervise practicum students. The role of the field instructor is challenging, complex, multi-faceted and has evolved in terms of process and practice expectations. The titles accorded this position vary, like those of the field education coordinator, and will be used interchangeably in this text. The field instructor can be referred to as the field supervisor, field teacher, field liaison and human services supervisor. The field instructor should be committed to her/his teaching role and be aware of "differentiated" knowledge relevant to the position and the profession. The position should hold equal status to that of a course director because of the teaching and evaluative responsibilities.

The practicum consists of several hundred hours, although this varies among schools. Since no other course provides such intimate contact between student and teacher, modelling is inherent in the practice/teaching function. Practice teachers value their role as educators and learners and receive scant appreciation within the organization. Despite the present climate of restraint and cutbacks, field instructors, by and large, are still providing excellent supervision and education to our students (Preston 1999). Most universities do not provide remuneration to agencies, and, therefore, having a practicum student adds to an already burdened work schedule.

Field instructors have noted the changing calibre of practicum students as schools are compelled to take more students to fill registration demands. Students are admitted with less experience, and they tend to have multiple responsibilities, especially in the area of employment and family. University cutbacks also infringe on the ability of the field department to sustain excellent learning sites; there is a high turnover of field instructors, which can often jeopardize students' learning. Although the duties of the field instructor have been well-documented in the literature, there are gaps in the research relating to teaching, understanding, knowing and effecting antiracist and anti-oppressive practice in preparing students to practise in a diverse global context. This chapter looks at the traditional role and functions of the field instructor through a brief historical review, with a view to inclusivity. An analysis of power, privilege, culture and identity allows for reflections on how location and position are constructed and produced to sustain dominant behaviours and practices. Through personal and professional reflections and understandings of how differentiated knowledge is produced, the field instructor can provide the space to engage the student in critical debates to effect antiracist and anti-oppressive perspectives.

HISTORICAL PERSPECTIVES OF FIELD LIAISON

A study conducted by Fortune and Abramson (1993) concluded that student satisfaction in the practicum depended on the relationship and skills of the field instructor. Marshack and Glassman (1991) outlined the historical role of the field instructor beginning with the "student's adoption of a supervisor's accumulated wisdom and its application to the learner's own practice" (86). When psychoanalysis was the major theoretical intervention, the student's personality was under scrutiny in order to promote and enhance effectiveness in practice. Systems theory, which included learning paradigms for both field instructor and student, was later introduced. Experiential approaches have also been utilized as a means of engaging in effective field instruction.

Cleak, Hawkins and Hess (2000) challenge the traditional model of field instruction, where the "clinical" model is still emphasized because of the one-to-one relationship with the field instructor within a particular agency. This approach is constraining and does not allow for innovation and challenge. Cleak et al. (2000) state that a more broad-based range of skills is needed in practice to respond to globalization and privatization (162). Flexible learning, collaboration, creativity and commitment, together with a diverse range of different teaching methods and learning experiences, will enhance student learning. Most agencies have developed an eclectic approach with the exception of those where there is a favoured model. Some of these prescribed approaches are brief therapy, narrative therapy and feminist and radical perspectives. While some students seek these specific sites to gain particular skills, others are prepared to shadow the field instructor and learn differential experiences. Practitioners tend to use intervention strategies from a range of theorists together with intuitive and deductive reasoning to arrive at working solutions.

According to Kadushin (1976), field instructing includes three different tasks: managing, educating and supporting, or, as Towle (1963) similarly states, administrative, teaching and helping. Wilson (2000) echoes these administration, educational and supportive functions but critically analyzes the tensions inherent in these functions. Questions and concerns have arisen in terms of the time assigned to each task component and which segment tends to be more critical. Administration refers to the organization and management of the field practicum for the student. Its tasks may include conducting pre-screening interviews, informing the staff about student participation, consulting with other staff to share duties, organizing orientation for the students, establishing a learning contract, attending seminars at the school, liaising and meeting with the faculty field liaison and scheduling and effecting time for supervision and evaluation. These are the expected tasks of the field instructor. However, if these administrative tasks are well-organized and implemented, there will be critical space for engaged dialogue about theory and practice.

The teaching and learning roles are very critical for a successful placement. Studies indicate that a major asset is the supervisor's ability to be attuned to the learning style and personal characteristics of the student so that assignments can be planned and difficulties can be anticipated (Choy et al. 1998). Students' learning capacity is increased if their learning style matches those of their supervisor. Likewise, being of the same gender leads to more positive evaluations (Behling, Curtis and Foster 1982). Supervisors need to be in touch with their own learning and teaching styles to critically analyze the learning style of the student in order to match suitable projects and to project outcomes in terms of the evaluation of skills and strengths. These observations are crucial to the supervisory process and can alleviate frustrations and misunderstandings. Van Soest and Kruzick (1994) state that the focus of the literature has been on the relationship between the behaviours of supervisor and student with little emphasis on how we teach and learn and how our different perspectives directly influence supervision (50). Cooper (2000) examines the nature of learning professional practice and emphasizes the need for supervisors to understand students and how they learn professional practice (10). She emphasizes the complementarity of teaching and learning in the role of field instructing. Monitoring the learning environment is also critical to provide feedback and evaluation. Bogo and Vayda (1998) emphasize helping students develop self-awareness but advise caution handling emotional difficulty, which should only be included in supervision insofar as it pertains to student learning.

Raskin (1982) notes that students relate more positively with field instructors who have skills and abilities in technical, evaluative and human relations areas. A field instructor needs to be attuned to the personal characteristics as well as the learning styles of their students. There are concrete skills which students expect of the field instructor in order to make their placement effective. According to Hagen (1989), students highly value organized orientation to the agency, formal teaching, skill development, supervision and case selection procedures. Are these areas of focus however sufficient to stretch students' abilities and potential for practice in the new millennium? Is the nature of professional social work practice limited to these traditional functions of the field instructor? I contend that these roles can be expanded to incorporate an anti-oppressive and antiracist analysis which allows us to rethink social work practice and education in the wake of the increasing use of technology and the proliferation of global trade.

Jarman-Rohde et al. (1997) state that socio-political issues, such as funding cuts and devolution of services, impact greatly on the ability of the field to respond to the needs of the student. Understanding diversity and difference is often an additive component in the learning experience within many agencies. Students who desire to practise from an anti-oppressive perspective and who view the larger structure as being implicated in dominance and privilege may have difficulty in achieving some of their learning goals. Smart and Gray (2000) discuss the implications of having a political and structural awareness of societal issues and the forces of oppression. Students needs to feel "safe" to discuss their insights and feelings on these issues. The shifting contexts of practice in terms of diversity and differences compel us to create safe space for discussions.

POWER DYNAMICS AND KNOWLEDGE PRODUCTION

The skills and knowledge outlined above are necessary for the field instructor to be effective, but a knowledge base, to ensure that an antiracist and anti-oppressive approach is actively taught, is also very important. Understanding issues relating to power, subjectivity and knowledge production within the field teacher/student relationship will lead to more effective practice, including ways to challenge oppression. As earlier stated, the field education coordinator needs to first begin with the self and understand forms of dominance, privilege and whiteness (see Chapter Two). These issues are also critical for the field instructor in the role of field teacher. The field instructor needs to have a sound knowledge base of systemic inequalities and be able to discuss issues relating to oppression with the student. This process is expected of all constituents managing the field, and it begins with a thorough knowledge of how the agency responds to issues about oppression and one's location within these structures. The field instructor also needs to be knowledgeable about the school curriculum in order to challenge and integrate the practice of theory in placement. In this era of late capitalism and globalization we are being constantly called upon to respond to a wide range of social issues in which race, class, gender, sexual orientation, age and ability are implicated. The field teacher/student relationship can be the springboard for discussion of such issues, since commonalities and differences exist between these two bodies.

De Montigny (1995) states that administrative demands dictate the daily practice of social workers, and their present location is derived from managed care and shifts in state and political power. He argues that:

> To do social work is to engage in socially organized practices of power: the power to investigate, to assess, to produce authorized accounts, to present case "facts" and to intervene in people's lives. The exercise of such power—is also realized through more subtle and less visible moments of practice. (209)

Power issues are inherent in every relationship since there are visible and underlying differences in terms of race and forms of oppression. The concept of power is integral to relational conceptions of identity and professionalism. Power is inscribed in dominant discourse, in student–teacher relationships, and in practice which denotes rigidity or determines inclusion and exclusion. Professionals exercise power over their clients when they use their own truths, their understandings, and their values to interpret the client's world. Beginning discussions of the discursive power of the client/counsellor encounters and the domination of institutional discourse helps us to understand how "colonizing the other" happens through claims of expert knowledge (Chambon and Irving 1998: xvii). In the same text, *Reading Foucault for Social Work,* Epstein (1999) refers to practice as "technical fix" while Irving (1999) calls for a "radical questioning" and "fearless thinking" in order to lead us to a more profound understanding of the world (29).

Wilson (2000) discusses the inherent tensions within the roles of administrating, educating and supporting. Balancing the student's needs with the agency functions, providing support and, at the same time, challenging the student's learning can lead to tensions. Wilson believes that these conflicts arise when there is a power imbalance between the student and field instructor (27). Field instructors occupy positions of power when they impose their knowledge and expectations on the students using a traditional theoretical lens, without acknowledging dominant discourse and problematizing subjective space. I agree with Rossiter (2000) who argues that we cannot be innocent and altruistic in our work. Applying the work of Foucault, she explains how workers appear to self-regulate and self-govern rather than appearing to be constrained within structures (150). Foucault (1980) explored the inseparability of power and knowledge by interrogating who is silenced through discourse. He claims that power comes from below, meaning from the subject, and that knowledge is claimed and internalized through every social interaction. Being part of a society allows this knowledge then to be claimed as truths, integrated and privileged. Claiming knowledge as truths depends on one's status in society; therefore, we are compelled to examine whose voice gets heard, whose knowledge gets privileged and whose voice is silenced. These exponential arguments force us to examine how knowledge is constructed in the field teacher/student relationship.

In the field instructor/student relationship, the supervisor is viewed as being the expert, having knowledge and skills which can be imparted to the student. Often the practitioner is viewed as the role model who embodies professionalism and expertise. The practitioners have largely been trained to integrate traditional white Euro-Western theories and operate within the standards set by the agency (Rossiter 2000). The historical legacies of the profession include colonization and imperialist practices. Gil (1998) states that contemporary manifestations of injustice and oppression, such as racism and sexism, have social, psychological, political and historical uniquenesses (27). However they also have common sources and interact and intersect to produce social relations. It is critical to connect contemporary forms of injustice to historical patterns of injustice such as genocide, slavery, anti-Semitism, poverty and other forms of oppression. We need to know how the present is intricately tied to history: we cannot be innocent of this knowledge in our daily work. Field instructors need to have conceptual understandings of economic imperialism, exploitation and domination, and seek to transform practice. If these realities are not present in the field instruction discourse the resulting silence and omission help to sustain power and subjugate knowledge. Rossiter (2000) clearly outlines this position by examining the therapist/client relationship, which mirrors that of the field instructor/student:

> we need to question the potential for reenactment of historical relations of inequality in every therapeutic encounter. Understanding the play of power in therapy requires intricate self-reflexiveness regarding how historical relations may be acted out between therapist and client. When there is an absence of radical doubt about relations between groups socialized within historical relations of inequality, then therapy can become a vehicle for recapitulating that history.... The focus must shift from "those" with power to "us," as we embody the micropolitics of power in our daily lives—through what we forget, what we permit, how we obey, how power works through our bodies, and how we foster regimes of truth. (159)

Field instructors have the potential for unravelling the interplay of power and practice and incorporating a socio-political and historical context in their work. Situating social work within a historical framework is especially significant in order to understand our imperial legacies and traditions. The political nature of social work is being carefully examined in texts (Mullaly 1997, Carniol 2000): they show that the legacies of paternalistic and colonized forms of caring have been deeply etched in social work's history. Margolin (1997) notes the gaze which we cast on our clients, a gaze which emphasizes the vulnerability of our clients. These critiques help to create a view of the dynamics inherent in the teacher/student relationship which ought to be reconsidered from an anti-imperialist and antiracist perspective.

The student who wants to practise within the mainstream and learn unproblematically from the traditional approach to field instructing may not encounter overt difficulties. Students who challenge mainstream thinking become more acutely attuned to ways in which their voices can be silenced and repressed. Students who desire to maintain and incorporate a political and anti-oppressive perspective in their practice may be faced with conflict and tension if the field instructor does not perceive these realities. The student who is aware of systemic oppression and is constrained within the agency can risk failing or being marginalized in the practicum (see Chapter Seven).

In this text I have outlined critical analyses of particular components of field education. Together with these critiques it is also helpful to review process and procedures needed to effect a change process. These concrete efforts should in no way deter the reader from a careful scrutiny of her/his role in perpetuating privilege, oppression and marginalization. Rather, the analysis of a concrete change process provides a simultaneous ground to test and challenge our shifting knowledge in order to produce new meanings to promote, teach and practice.

THINKING THROUGH A CHANGE PROCESS

Field instructors need to be attuned to the exigencies of practice in terms of an analytical understanding of race and oppression. As stated earlier, the danger of omission can be detrimental to the student and the client. Students report great anxiety about the practicum course (Rompf, Royse and Dhooper 1993); this anxiety can be further exacerbated for minority students in placement if there is a denial of differences and subtle and/or blatant forms of discrimination. Since the field instructor has a powerful influence on the student as a professional (Bogo and Vayda 1987, Shulman 1983, Schneck, Grossman and Glassman 1991), she/he should ensure that students have appropriate orientation to the placement setting in order to minimize anxiety and possible feelings of exclusion.

The role of the field instructor within the program is critical to facilitate change and growth especially in areas demanding personal and professional commitment. First, field instructors should begin the process of inclusivity in the pre-screening interview by ensuring that there is a discussion about work with diverse populations and the agency's mandate concerning anti-harassment and sexual exploitation. Moreover students should feel empowered to inquire about practice and supervisory process in the area of diversity. This discussion should not only take place with those with marginalized status but with all students who challenge their location within dominant spaces. During this interview the instructor can begin to discuss the politics of practice through an introduction of the policies within the agency, anti-harassment and anti-oppression procedures, and her/his own location within dominant structures.

Second, field instructors must be attuned to the position of the student within oppressive structures. In a multiculturally diverse city it is a harsh reminder of oppression when the agency does not reflect the ethnoracial composition of the community. It is also critical that the agency reflect other forms of diversity among the staff. Students from minority groups have to face great hurdles within institutions where there is silence and lack of opportunities to discuss issues relating to oppression. Students who come from lower socio-economic backgrounds may feel further marginalized when they are faced with clients and situations that relate to poverty and homelessness.

Third, it is incumbent on the field instructor to introduce topics relating to antiracist and anti-oppressive practice at the interview in order to indicate acceptance of the student and an openness to political discourse. Minority students have difficulty broaching topics relating to oppression for fear of being marginalized and rejected even in the prescreening interview. The instructor needs to allow for discussions of values and ideology, and critical thinking about societal inequities as they impinge on theory and practice.

Fourth, field instructors are invited to attend seminars at the school of social work during the course of their role with students. Seminar presenters can be asked to include an analysis of racism and oppression as it relates to their topic, while the coordinator should provide information pertaining to the philosophy and expectations of the department. Presenters should include field instructors, faculty, community workers and students; the topics should reflect current practice issues. Our seminars have resulted in lively discussions that create further opportunities for inclusive practice. Our university is located in a large metropolis and agencies are shared among three area universities and also colleges. As a result, there is a huge turnover with field instructors and agencies, which makes long-term planning challenging. The seminars have been a successful educational alternative.

Over the past year I have facilitated workshops, presented at seminars and participated in discussions that were focused on the theme of anti-oppression principles in field education. These situations have been uncomfortable because the participants, whether minority or non-minority, were divided on the advisability of beginning a discourse about anti-oppressive practice at the pre-screening interview. According to Williams (1991), "the cold game of equality staring" becomes stark and burdensome when facilitating such discourse. Field instructors felt that a discussion of antiracism/oppression would make the minority student feel marginalized. Some minority field instructors and students concurred. It is obvious that the context and construction of new ideas and approaches need further deliberation. To simply acknowledge the colour of a student in an initial interview without awareness and education about inclusivity would indeed be marginalizing and very disconcerting. During, and more intensely after, these workshops I felt uneasy and disheartened with the learning paradigm about oppression.

This internal struggle persisted because I remembered my experiences as a minority student where there was a denial of my cultural identity; yet my otherness was felt very sharply on a daily basis—in the classroom, at the field interview and at my mainstream placement. My initial disappointment at the first few workshops stemmed from the fact that the majority field instructors did not recognize the denial that existed within themselves about issues of oppression or how deeply the experience of oppression is felt within marginalized groups. Also, as minority workers and students, we have had to learn from theorists whose pedagogical principles and cognitive awareness did not include an understanding of the lives of marginalized groups in society. As a result, we have either become so immersed in an oppressive system that it becomes too tiresome to continue to challenge for change, or we may have internalized our oppression so deeply that current approaches to practice are seen as effective measures for competency as a social worker. Oppressive practices are manifested in subtle, and even blatant, ways in placement. For example, students may be assigned only clients who belong to their own ethnic groups. Although these students may prefer working with their own groups, it is important for field instructors to discuss preferences with the students before making such an assumption. Smart and Gray (2000) observe how minority students suffer discrimination and "play the game" rather than challenge the system, which can be exhausting and depressing. They outline some principles for field instructors to use in working with minority students (106). Some of these are openness, flexibility, sensitivity, recognizing limited knowledge of oppression, personal awareness and respect for the students' values and attitudes. As well, the instructor should show an appreciation of spirituality, an understanding of racism, oppression, socio-political forces, history and colonization. The instructor should also be able to question traditional models of supervision and be open to developing alternative approaches (105–106). These are examples of the kind of issues inherent in our discussions at all seminars.

Fifth, it is critical that field instructors pay attention to the language and behaviours which may be part of the culture of the agency. Many times students report their disillusionment when the incidental chatter of workers includes casual derogatory remarks about particular clients and families. Students report that they feel powerless to challenge their field instructors/supervisors or other agency personnel for fear of backlash because of the power differential and the evaluative nature of placements. Students who are members of the group that is the target of oppression will feel judged and devalued by the negative comments.

Sixth, field instructors must be helped to feel comfortable to discuss organizational issues including the political reality, related to funding constraints, of increasing caseloads. Workers face burnout and feel abused and oppressed within a system over which they also feel powerless. Our field instruction seminars provide opportunities to discuss several of these issues and could be easily integrated at educational events in field education departments.

CONCLUSION

Field instructors are the teachers in the practicum course. Although there are several institutional layers involved in this course delivery, the impact of this role is enormous. Since the placement consists of several hundred hours, field instructors have the power to help students shape their professional identity. There is rich opportunity to engage in debates about power, privilege and knowledge production in order for students to challenge the environment of practice. To facilitate such discussions the field instructor needs to have a critical understanding of societal inequalities and the many faces of oppression. The analysis should incorporate knowledge of the historical imperial legacies of the profession and how we are implicated within repressive structures. Transformative knowledge to incorporate justice and inclusion means an unsettling of the hegemonic practice approaches to allow for interrogations of theoretical underpinnings and practice interventions. It is no longer acceptable to practise from an innocent location.

Chapter Six

The Integrative Seminar as a Pedagogical Tool for Anti-oppressive Social Work Field Education[1]

The integrative seminar is an integral component of the practicum course and complements other educational initiatives. The historical objectives of the seminar have been to provide a space for students to discuss the integration of theory and practice; to promote peer support; to share knowledge about community resources; to question ethics and practice; to examine responses to clients and situations; to debate social policy issues; and to analyze administration and organizational structures. The integrative seminar is conducted either as another course running concurrently with the field practicum (Mok 1993) or as a series of planned sessions during the student practicum (Bogo and Vayda 1987). Roles and responsibilities should be well defined, and the benefits should be clearly determined, clarified and outlined so that there is some consistency in the approach, form and content.

There are additional challenges which students can bring to these seminars for discussion. For example, many students find it difficult to incorporate political and structural components of social work at their placement site. The seminar can allow for discussions of oppression inherent in agency politics and reflections of professional identity. The students can also engage in critical discourse to enhance professional and innovative antiracist and anti-oppressive practice. This seminar provides pedagogical and practice benefits for the student and instructor. Given the shifting nature of practice, there should also be mechanisms to provide feedback to ensure that the seminars are in fact allowing for progressive and innovative discussions about practice.

This chapter begins with analyses of current practices of integrative seminars. There is scant information about this topic, yet most schools have some form of concurrent seminar or class with the practicum. More attention is given to the integration of theory and practice, the pedagogical abilities of field instructors and students' learning environment. The cognitive and scholarly aspects of field instruction seminars are not carefully or extensively explored. These seminars can be an effective pedagogical and learning tool for social work field education. The following analysis includes a reflection of one school's deliberations about, and experiences with, introducing the integrative seminar to the field curriculum. A working model for the integrative seminar will be discussed, taking into account the student concerns, the literature, present social realities and informal feedback from faculty and students. It is important to build a framework to accommodate the ongoing and pressing social and political issues which arise during student placement. Implications for innovative approaches to conducting and facilitating these seminars will be highlighted: they need to be responsive to the needs of the students, to consider the distinctive pedagogical style of the faculty and to promote a critical anti-oppressive framework for practice.

SOME REFLECTIONS

The integrative seminar was introduced in our school approximately five years ago during the restructuring and organizing of the field education process to reflect the critical anti-oppressive approach of our revised curriculum. Visits to the field were reduced from three to one with the proviso that students attend two seminars each term for the course of their placement. Our B.S.W. program is a part-time one: students can begin the practicum in the spring, fall or winter term and fulfill the placement hours in anywhere from two to five days. While this flexibility works well for some agencies and our students, planning and organizing can be very problematic. Students do not begin and end as a group, as in most schools; therefore, organizing continued learning opportunities poses problems. A four-year B.S.W. program begins in the fall of 2002, and therefore students will be placed as a group rather than at different times throughout their part-time study.

Faculty members felt that the seminars were a more educative alternative to the three field visits which became social visits by the third round. Also, the time to negotiate three field visits, given our vast geographic area, was problematic. Visits were reduced to one, and more as required. The seminars were introduced after deliberations about structure, content and process; all faculty members were committed to the change. Implementing the integrative seminar was therefore critical to allow the students to link with their peers, promote collaboration, and share knowledge about theory in practice.

Over the years, however, the purpose and pedagogical benefits of these seminars began to be questioned by faculty and students. Students felt that they had to travel long distances to come to the seminars, and they reported that a major part of the time was spent on introductions and sharing stories rather than in-depth discussions about practice issues. Some faculty members questioned the pedagogical benefits of the seminars, and students were indicating ways to improve the seminars on their final evaluation form. Over the years students began shifting from one seminar to the next when their schedule did not fit with the seminar time with their own faculty advisor. These shifts resulted in disjointedness and inconsistencies. These were the more concrete structural issues of one school and could be more easily remedied. What was more important was the need to construct a solid analytical framework for faculty and students that would assist all schools to promote this vehicle for learning. It must also be noted that faculty have different pedagogical styles and approaches. Some faculty members had consistently positive reviews and comments from students about dynamic discussions about critical practice. Other students indicated that they derived more benefit from peer support and from becoming more knowledgeable about different contexts of practice.

What appeared to be lacking at these seminars was a framework to promote the educative benefits, such as recognizing the production and practice of theory and the ways in which these seminars could promote critical global perspectives. The feedback of students and faculty indicated that our approach had severe limitations and we felt that improvements could be made to maximize the potential benefits of this learning opportunity. The following study resulted from this feedback, which created an urgency to examine our current style and format. A student survey provided information for us to establish some guidelines to enhance the design, content and approach. This study also includes an in-depth analysis of the "Student Evaluation of the Practicum Forms" and informal conversations and discussions with students and faculty.

It is important to acknowledge that the process and design of integrative seminars in each school will continue to differ. What is critical in this chapter is the need to pay attention to this semi-organized space for students to engage in discourses about global practice issues. As Jarman-Rohde et al. (1997) state, "one critical component of a unified curriculum is the integrative seminar" (43). Ongoing evaluation from student and faculty will assist in measuring the effectiveness of these seminars and in seeking ways to enhance pedagogical and practice applications. Undoubt-edly other schools may have well-designed approaches to this educative tool. However, a search of the literature did not provide a comprehensive analysis of this practicum component, hence the need to explore and examine ways to promote this seminar and ensure that it integrates a critical antidiscriminatory approach.

PREVIOUS RESEARCH AND ANALYSES

As stated in other chapters, the literature on the organization of field education in general is sparse. Wilson et al. (2001) provide a detailed approach to incorporating the integrative seminar into the graduate pro-gram over a period of five years. Their analysis led to a semi-structured, student-driven curriculum which demanded case scenario presentations and discussions. The meagre literature on the integrative seminar primarily deals with the integration of theory and practice. Integrating theory with practice has been the topic of numerous articles and texts (e.g., Sheafor and Jenkins 1982, Bogo and Vayda 1987, Marshack and Glassman 1991, Norberg and Schneck 1991, Goldstein 1993, Rabin, Sabaya and Frank 1994). The challenge of integrating theory and practice remains the gist of academic inquiry (Mok 1993, Coady 1995). Jordan (1982) has explored the merits of the integration of theory and practice, while Coady (1995) suggests the need to be comfortable with these ongoing challenges; he promotes a "reflective-inductive" model for this integration. His explora-tion of the research indicated that practitioners may not apply theory in their practice to the extent that we assume. Instead many practitioners use "reflection, spontaneity, intuition and 'inductive reasoning' rather than the conscious application of theoretical skills and techniques" (142). This particular study indicates that reasoning, reflecting, analyzing and using moral judgement and experiences assist practitioners in actually "doing" their work. What is critical to recognize in this analysis is the reliance on the personal responses and knowledge of the worker. If the practitioner does not have a critical analysis and knowledge of the realities of racism and oppression and only relies on limited personal responses, then there is potential disservice and damage to the client because issues of culture, identity, race and oppression may be ignored or erased.

Vayda and Bogo (1991) cite the historical interest in the integration of classroom and field education and state that these debates are not about to go away. They indicate that as early as 1897 Richmond realized that practice must be supported by theory. The authors have developed the

"Integration of Theory and Practice Loop" to assist field instructors in their efforts to help students integrate theory and practice. They have extended this model to the classroom utilizing a holistic view in which concrete experience is followed by observation, reflection and formulation of hypotheses to be tested, thus creating new experience and professional responses (274). It is important to ensure that at each juncture there are critical questions relating to subjectivity, power, privilege and domination in the client/worker dynamic. More recently, Jarman-Rhode et al. (1997) pointed to the need for all schools to implement integrative seminars to augment leaning and allow students to think critically about their field experiences (43). Students are generally anxious and apprehensive about their practice skills and feel incompetent when they cannot aptly fit a theoretical perspective to the problem they are facing with their client or community. The seminar can provide the space to share these concerns, be validated by their peers and be further challenged (Fusco 1995).

Mok (1993) discusses a cognitive approach to linking theory and practice through the integrative seminar. He assumes the importance of this objective in the profession and proposes steps to achieve this goal through the integrative seminar which is taught as an academic course. The author prescribes the tasks of the course with clearly delineated content and methods for integrated learning, ending with a final examination. While the author experiences the "cognitive" in this approach, the mechanisms to achieve understanding of theory/practice integration are all prescriptive. In this analysis there are no attempts to create a "liberated space" to engage and dialogue about differences. Constructive critical analysis was only allowed during student presentations. Obviously there are distinct approaches to this educative practice component. What is not clearly outlined is the rich opportunity to produce meanings in this seminar for transformative and innovative social work practice.

Theory and practice dilemmas are relevant to the discussion since theory and practice inform each other. Modern technology and transnational alliances with corporations and governments have resulted in the restructuring and downsizing of agencies and institutions where many social workers are employed. Rapid movement of people across the globe has also created shifts in population locations and multicultural societies challenge the traditional theoretical approaches of social work. Efforts to understand diversity and oppression demand attention and discussion. Field education is responding to these changes through inclusion of diversity issues and cross-cultural training (Van Soest 1996, Razack, Teram and Rivera 1995, Summers and Yellow Bird 1995). Anti-oppression and antiracist models are also emerging (Dominelli 1991, Macey and Moxon 1996). Field education needs to pay continued attention to shifting social contexts: it should develop programs to facilitate discussion about global issues. The integrative seminars provide the opportunity to promote such discourses.

Gonsales Del Valle et al. (1991) utilizes a transcultural and empowerment approach in the practicum, as a way to bring students to accept the positive characteristics of cultural identity and differences through a "dialectical method of education and professional practice that integrates conflict theory and liberation education principles" (47). This design is guided by a separate committee to ensure that all constituents of the practicum and of this transcultural model are integrated into the school curriculum. Salcido et al. (1995) conducted research to explore the effects of utilizing a cross-cultural training model in the integrative seminar. The findings revealed that cross-cultural training combined with experiential exercises have a greater effect on students acquiring skills in practice.

The integrative seminar allows for students to discuss critical issues about their field practice in an atmosphere where the primary focus is not on evaluation but largely on peer support and skill building, which emerge through animated group discussions with fellow students. The seminars need not only focus on traditional concerns such as theory/practice issues but should move beyond these binaries to more engaged, fluid discussions about practice. At these seminars students often complain about their lack of practice skills and consistently want to know "how to" or seek a recipe to respond to social ills. As Freire (1990) states, "students should have a critical permanent curiosity toward the world" (7). He exhorts students to move away from "the pedagogy of the answer." Likewise Parton (2000) argues for us to theorize the uncertainties and ambiguities inherent in the profession rather than seeking to define and measure procedures in practice.

At the integrative seminar, students have another avenue to further theorize from their particular perspective and to create synergy from their differing contexts. This forum helps students to use their shared experiences to validate their feelings, be challenged about their approaches and engage in mutual problem-solving processes. Students can also discuss tensions arising in the field resulting from varied tasks, abilities, organizational structures and procedures, and personal values and beliefs (Walden and Brown 1985). The instructors in these seminars also act as the field liaison for the students, so they are familiar with their student's practicum settings. The sharing of field experiences at these seminars exposes the students to a wide range of social work settings, methods, theories and client groups (Conklin and Borecki 1991). Guidelines to achieve the above can be difficult to facilitate if the seminars are not structured appropriately and if there is also no space for faculty to discuss and share their varied experiences and approaches.

In a very diverse global society, the ground for practice is constantly shifting and, based on the subjective nature of practice, there will always be the need to share and discuss our individual ways of making meanings in our work. Social work does not have a template to respond to individual people's life situations. While there have been efforts to standardize assessments and intervention plans, the social and subjective location of the worker continues to be a focal point of discussion. Critical anti-oppressive perspectives need to be considered from personal and professional standpoints. The integrative seminar provides the space for such a dialogue.

RESEARCH METHOD

In this section the various approaches utilized to collect information for analysis of the integrative seminar will be discussed. I began with a survey, which was conducted with students who had completed their practica during the past two years, to determine the effectiveness of this pedagogical tool. A total of 114 questionnaires were mailed to students and sixty-two usable questionnaires were returned. The response rate was 54.4 percent . Information from the questionnaire was entered into the computer for analysis. Open-ended responses were entered into a word processor. This study will be analyzed in conjunction with feedback from student evaluation forms, faculty observations and informal discussions.

RESULTS OF THE SURVEY

The sixty-two students who responded to our survey were placed in a diverse range of settings, including child and family services, hospitals, mental health facilities, ethno-cultural agencies, corrections, shelters and substance abuse programs. Most students (93.3 percent) rated their satisfaction with the selection of their practica as "fair to excellent." From the perspective of the practicum as a learning experience, 96.8 percent rated theirs as "good to excellent." Satisfaction with the degree of preparation the students felt they had received from the school's curriculum did not rank as high. A total of 65.4 percent rated their preparation as "good to excellent," while 34.4 percent reported it as only "fair" and the remainder (8.2 percent) as "poor." The curriculum can be a source of tension for students when they begin the practicum since they look for a prescriptive fit with the issues and problems they face with their client group.

With regard to the integrative seminars, students said they attended anywhere from one to five sessions (mean=2.4). The number of students in each session ranged from two to fifteen (mean=7.9). Table 1 presents the topics discussed within these seminars. As indicated, most (87.1 percent) students reported that they had an opportunity to share their practicum experiences with other students in these seminars. Supervision was also commonly discussed and students felt this area of focus was somewhat helpful. In terms of the usefulness of the various topics, most felt the opportunity to share their experiences and hear from other students was the most helpful aspect of the integrative seminars.

Table 1
Topics Discussed in Integrative Seminars and Rankings of Helpfulness to Students

	Yes	No	Rank*
Experiences in Practicum	87.1	12.9	1
Practicum Supervision	64.5	35.5	4
Impact of Cutbacks	38.7	61.3	5
Issues of Oppression	35.5	64.5	3
Theory in Relation to Practice	35.5	64.5	2
Case Presentations	32.3	67.7	3
Learning Contracts	32.3	67.7	6
Methods of Intervention	27.4	72.6	4
Evaluation of Practicum	22.6	77.4	7
Total = 100%; N = 62			
* Ranking of "Helpfulness" to students			

Thirty-five percent of students indicated that they had discussed issues pertaining to oppression: the overall rank of this in terms of helpfulness indicated the need to pay further attention to this area. Discussion of theory in relation to practice drew similar scores and ranked second in terms of importance, and the opportunities to present and discuss particularly difficult cases and situations in placement were also viewed by the students as being significant. Supervision and methods of intervention were viewed as being somewhat helpful to discuss, while the other areas were found to be less important.

STUDENT EVALUATION OF THE PRACTICUM FORMS

Students' evaluation of the practicum forms also provided input into this study. A Practicum Task Force Committee was spearheaded in 1999 to review the practicum, since we were cognizant that our current process was not effective and were seeking feedback for change. Preston (1999) conducted a review of the Student Evaluation of the Practicum Forms, looking at approximately 539 evaluation forms collected over a four-year period, 1995–1999. The findings confirmed our observations that the integrative seminar needed to be reconceptualized in order to be effective. Students referred to the disjointedness when other students joined their group. Since some travelled long distances to attend, when there was a loose structure and little in-depth discussions of theory or practice issues, they felt angry and cheated. They complained about redundancy, repetition of material presented and lack of information about critical practice issues. Although positive feedback outweighed the negative responses, it was evident that we needed to make changes.

The benefits validated what was already known to some degree. Hearing others' stories about their work was important as well as learning about other agencies and resources. Those student who felt isolated in their placement connected with their peers at these seminars, and they all felt validated and supported when varied experiences were shared. They discussed the benefits of theory and practice integration and appreciated the link with the school and faculty, networking, shared job opportunities and having a "safe" space to share struggles. At these seminars there is a marked absence of excitement, curiosity and challenge, and/or interrogations about the profession of social work as it is situated within oppression and dominance. Is there then a lack of challenge at these seminars because of the short time allotment? Is there a concerted effort by faculty and student to discuss subjectivity, professional identity, surveillance in the workplace, organization and administrative structures, diversity, racism and oppression in practice? Has this space traditionally been marked for maintaining the dominant status quo to facilitate the integration of Eurocentric and western traditional theory and practice?

INFORMAL DISCUSSIONS WITH FACULTY

Faculty were initially excited and committed to facilitating these seminars: they still see the benefits of this learning component of the practicum. As stated earlier, many students described the dynamic discussions about the challenge of practice which they experienced at these seminars with their faculty advisors. Some faculty members consistently provided constructive feedback to the coordinator. However, all faculty members had similar concerns about the structure and organization of the seminars. Some felt that the disjointedness did not allow for engaged and dynamic discussion, while others shared a deeper concern about the need for a critical framework to understand the pedagogical benefits in conducting these seminars. These concerns led to this study—ultimately changes will be made to the structure and organization of these seminars. What is missing is a framework to assist faculty to realize the critical pedagogical and learning aspects of the integrative seminar.

DISCUSSION

Based on the survey results, Student Evaluation of the Practicum Forms, literature review and informal discussions with faculty, it was concluded that there is a need to establish some guidelines to maximize the effectiveness of the integrative seminar. While the survey responses reveal what areas are useful for discussion, feedback from Student Evaluations of the Practicum Forms indicates that seminars, which have focused on introduction and sharing experiences, could provide more critical analyses, discussion of issues and skill-building opportunities. Although there are many positive responses to indicate the merit of running integrative seminars concurrently with the practicum, the loosely adapted format can prove to be meaningless for many students and even for the instructor, who may hold the belief that pedagogical opportunities are nil. Students, who take time off from their placement in order to attend the seminars, may be disillusioned if no effort is put into the organization, structure and content. Again, some of the more concrete changes in the structure and organization of the seminars are unique to our school. We are now offering four seminars to practicum students, and there will be ongoing revisions.

It is important to state that organizing and providing a framework for discussion of critical issues will not imperil notions of academic freedom for the seminar instructor: style and pedagogical approach, which will always be unique to the individual, can assist the instructor in the beginning process and allow for flexibility in the design. Although a seminar should not be teacher-driven, there are ways to introduce critical issues for discussion so that students can be informed and conscious of their professional role. For example, recently there have been reports about the status of child poverty, homelessness and changes to immigration policy. As well, in the aftermath of September eleventh, we need to challenge our thinking about global politics. These issues can be introduced for awareness and analysis relating to justice and equity. The format, therefore, should allow for innovation, be student-driven and practice-related.

It seems clear that students need a forum to discuss how their academic and personal experiences relate to their practicum. These areas include attention to anti-oppression and theory in relation to practice issues and a space to discuss their related struggles in their practicum work settings. It is important, therefore, to outline a framework and organize a process for ensuring that the integrative seminars reflect the needs of the participants and have relevance for social work practice. The top three themes indicated by the students are interrelated and will be incorporated in the framework for the seminar. In order to develop and sustain effective pedagogical approaches and a flexible structure for integrative seminars, these three areas will be highlighted: to construct the agenda at the first seminar where the guidelines for peer sharing can be discussed; to critically debate practice dilemmas; and to discuss anti-oppression principles from socio-political perspectives.

THE FIRST SEMINAR: CONSTRUCTING THE FORMAT AND SETTING THE AGENDA

Some of the major items for consideration at the first seminar relate to the process of placement, and these areas should be given brief mention since this information is usually included in practicum manuals. These issues include administrative procedures, goals and learning objectives/contract, supervision and evaluation, and the commitment and roles of all the constituents. Some time should be spent on student introductions: seminar instructors can make these introductions more meaningful by attaching importance to networking, to learning from others' experiences and to the varied practice modalities at their placement sites. Different approaches to social work could be highlighted and discussed. Students can also reflect on the various employment opportunities inherent in the profession. During these in-depth introductions, the facilitator can help to make links with agency and discuss practice modalities and other shared concerns. The seminar instructor can assist students to adopt a critical, analytical, reflective analysis of issues they bring to the discussion. The seminar instructor can also discuss the benefits of peer groups and encourage students to begin forming parallel cultures of support outside the institution.

It is at the practicum where many students begin to identify with the profession and/or struggle with their roles as social workers. Some also question their choices in terms of practice settings and begin to reflect on their abilities and skills. The role of the seminar instructor includes helping the student to make the links with practice, engaging students in examining organizational policies and structure, and encouraging them to begin to challenge their roles and philosophy about practice. At the end of the first seminar, the students should be encouraged to raise critical practice issues arising from their placement and organize a discursive presentation focusing on the practicum experience. It is also incumbent on the faculty advisor to remind students of the importance of incorporating anti-oppression principles into the analyses of their experiences in placement. Students can be encouraged to be knowledgeable about the mandate of the agency and its policies and procedures, especially about harassment and racism. They should observe the diversity in the workplace, clientele, staff and board of directors. Although students may have discussed the practicalities of these issues in the classroom, the reality is that when they are faced with the challenge of the work, attention to structural issues gets minimized.

THEORIZING PRACTICE

Theory in relation to practice was rated highly in terms of an important topic for discussion at the seminar. Although much has been written on the area of the integration of theory and practice (Tsang 1998), there is still an elusive quality to this concept. The integration of theory and practice is a misnomer that should be deconstructed in order to allay fears and refocus the debate about skills to one of ideology, construction of approaches and recognition of the links between the personal, the political and the educational as they emerge in practice. Research studies indicate that students in placement rarely relate to the theoretical skills learned in the classroom (Syson and Baginsky 1981). The goal of education in social work has been to equip the student with theories and skills which would be transferable to practice situations. It is rather obvious that such positivistic notions of education for practice are limiting since students in placements believe that they should have a grab bag of diverse theories to apply to practice situations. Tsang (1998) asked, "What is integration of theories and practice when one is uncertain of the meaning of the term 'social work theories?'" (171). It is more beneficial for the student to engage in debates, reflections and critical analyses of situations in order to understand what constitutes effective intervention in practice. Such critical and analytical thought would allow students to feel comfortable to analyze situations and learn how their personal ideology, together with a firm theoretical knowledge and skills base, would impact on particular situations.

Tsang (1998) stated that theories and knowledge "served as a guide for analysis and action, a model for practice, [and] a tool for understanding human behaviour and feelings" (172), while Harrison (1987) found that theories assist the student to develop and construct creative ways to work with clients (395). The seminars, therefore, should provide the space for students to discuss this issue, so that they are not overwhelmed by the illusion of incompetence or ignorance about their inability to fit definitive theories into particular practice situations. Fook, Ryan and Hawkins (1997), in their study of the nature of social work expertise, found that the use of theory was not articulated in positivistic terms. They found that social workers tended, instead, to rely on underlying assumptions, using particular concepts, and on developing a wisdom through intuition, rather than through articulated and integrated theoretical frameworks (407). The challenge for students is to understand the complexities of practice but not get bogged down with fitting a particular theory to a situation. Technocratic and positivistic formulas for practice situations produce anxieties in practice where, instead, there is a need for a distillation of ideas relating to the moral, ethical and humanistic dimensions of social work practice. Seminar instructors should be knowledgeable about such struggles and assist students to discuss these dilemmas.

Another important aspect relating to theory–practice debates is the tension which lies between the expectations of managers and administrators in the field and those of the academic institution. Students often discuss their incapacity to provide the theoretical underpinnings for practice: at field instruction seminars we frequently hear the instructors wish for the students to be more equipped with practice skills. Academics, on the other hand, focus on intellectual abilities to critically analyze, assess, critique and generate new ways of interpreting situations (Witkin 1998). These power struggles are diminishing as social work agencies and social work schools create more links for research and practice opportunities. Seminars for field instructors can be helpful in providing opportunities for discussion about some of these struggles. Since these dilemmas are especially crucial for students to discuss, the seminar instructor needs to be cognizant of the conflicts and explore ways in which these dichotomies can be contained.

Students and instructor must also be prepared to redefine social work, given present realities and contexts for practice. For example, if some students are engaged in political activity at the placement and are able to critically evaluate organizational process and structures, the seminar instructor can use their experience as teaching opportunities. Although generally students are still eager to have a prescribed format for doing social work, it is imperative for the seminar instructor to help them to recognize that they are engaging in theorizing practice through their experiential analyses and interventions.

ANTI-OPPRESSION PRINCIPLES ORGANIZED
FROM SOCIO-POLITICAL PERSPECTIVES

It is critical to incorporate issues of oppression within the discussions at every seminar. However, it can also be very difficult for seminar instructors to integrate such discussions. Razack, Teram and Rivera (1995) discussed the effectiveness of bi-weekly group discussions with students in placement, where an instructor facilitates discussions about systemic inequalities in practice. These seminars produced anxieties and tensions, yet forced students to question their own location when working with people from different cultures. Social work students, faculty and practitioners must constantly address the implications of social power, control and oppression in society and recognize the links to practice. While most students are exposed to such discussions in the classroom, their concern is that there is often little opportunity to engage in critical debate at the agency about anti-oppressive and political practice. The mention of anything political is met with suspicion, and advocacy in practice is not sufficiently encouraged. Practitioners negotiate their way in a system where the social safety net is being eroded and agencies struggle for survival. On the other hand, there are increased travel, trade and technological innovations, which make for a more intimate world, where global analysis of social issues becomes more relevant and where anti-oppressive constructs can be more fully examined.

It is our knowledge of these structures and our understandings of how we are complicit in maintaining power and privilege that are important in analyzing social issues. Students ought to be encouraged to recognize social justice initiatives and loopholes in the system relating to discrimination and oppression. They may begin in their agencies by examining policies, recruitment and hiring principles, the community being served or denied service and particular practice approaches. Since the facilitator's role is critical to this process, she/he should not only acknowledge privilege and power but also must possess expertise and skills in the area of anti-oppression as well as grounded analyses of race, racism, sexism, homophobia, ableism and ageism.

At our school the emphasis on critical thinking and social justice issues often results in anxiety for the student and for the practitioner/supervisor in situations where such debates are not introduced or encouraged. However, the community is awakening to the need to adopt a critical antiracist and anti-oppressive approach to practice, to allow for differences, to include a political dimension to the work and to examine entrenched structures. Anti-oppression and political practice are key areas of focus in any seminar and should therefore be incorporated in the framework.

CONTINUED ANALYSIS

This framework is a guide for building effective integrative seminars. These seminars constitute pedagogical components of social work field education since they provide the space to discuss challenging social issues without the fear of evaluation and judgement by a supervisor. Although the faculty member/instructor is present, there should be initial ground rules to understand the process. This understanding does not mean that racist, sexist, homophobic and other oppressive language and behaviours will be tolerated or ignored. Rather, students can identify how they are engaging in effecting an antidiscriminatory approach in their practice and describe some of the struggles and roadblocks.

It is also incumbent on faculty members to follow guidelines within their school in order to produce knowledge and learning at these forums. Although there is a respect for academic freedom and unique pedagogical approaches, engagement in critical anti-oppressive approaches to practice should be the underlying theme. Student evaluation of, and feedback from, these seminars is essential, and should be ongoing to maintain excellence in field education. Faculty should also be kept abreast of these evaluations so there is some accountability built in to the facilitator's role at these seminars. Efforts must be made through political debates to facilitate continued understandings of oppression and marginalization and the crucibles relating to the binary of theory/practice. There must be time allotted to share with new faculty the school's philosophy and approach as well as the design of the integrative seminar.

Conclusion

The integrative seminar is an important component of field education. Although these seminars have been introduced in many schools, the organization, structure and content of these seminars are not usually measured or evaluated for production of change. These seminars can provide critical and meaningful learning opportunities for students and instructor. Students engaging in the practicum need a space to be able to discuss issues relevant to their placement, build peer support and identify resources to assist them in their work. A framework for seminar instructors is therefore helpful to guide this process.

At the beginning of the first seminar it is imperative for the instructor to set the tone by attending to initial administrative details as well as sharing and allaying student anxieties about the work and the structures in which they operate. It is also critical to allow students to analyze their personal ideologies about practice and their beginning roles as professionals. Constructing the agenda together with the student at the first seminar is very important, since it allows them to raise practice and organizational issues. The seminar instructor needs to understand the anxieties that students face in their placement, as well as the structures in which they operate, in order to engage in debates about the challenges of theory/practice. It is important for the student to understand the concept of theory in practice and to look at how theory is created and shaped to fit present realities.

More importantly, the integrative seminar should also allow students to analyze the significance of understanding their ideology and their beginning role as a professional. It is also critical to facilitate discussions about the nature of anti-oppressive practice by allowing the students to bring in examples of struggles and positive work space to illustrate these dynamics. The role of the instructor is therefore critical for the seminar to be meaningful for, and challenging to, the practicum students. These seminars are especially crucial for hearing the voices of marginalized students, since their realities/differences become more distinct in the practicum setting.

Note

1. This paper was initially co-authored with Grant Macdonald, Associate Professor, School of Social Work, York University. We acknowledge the graduate assistant to this project, Shelley Hodder.

Chapter Seven

Marginality and Resistance:
Views from Oppressive Locations

The practicum can be a site of struggle for many students. If the reasons behind such struggle are not critically examined, the effects can be devastating for those involved. Life crises or traumatic events during the practicum can remind some students of their own oppression; this can cause difficulties. Some students may also view the time allotment for practicum as burdensome, due to family and employment responsibilities. Others, who encounter daily forms of oppression simply because of societal labels placed on them, may also experience challenges, causing significant stress and risk. Students who are gay, lesbian, living with a disability, from diverse racial and ethnic backgrounds and/or battle the stigmas of mental health problems may find the workplace intolerant, rigid and inflexible. These students, who endure struggles starting with the planning and organizing phase, may carry their fears and anxieties with them into the placement setting. This process can be demeaning and burdensome since the climate of acceptance can alter if oppression rears its ugly head. Likewise, field educators struggle with students who display weak interpersonal skills and have limited ability to apply conceptual skills in practice situations. The field educator, student, agency and school are all inextricably involved when there are concerns in the practicum.

This chapter focuses on five particular categories of student who face potential risks and whose struggles may create concerns and anxieties for field educators:

- racial minority students
- students with disabilities
- sexual minority students
- students with emotional/psychological problems
- mature students or experienced learners

[handwritten margin note: ASKED WHY INTERESTED HOMOSEXUAL COUPLES. MADE POINT TO SAY SHE ISN'T]

Implications for field education and social work practice are discussed and practical suggestions are outlined for the field educator, staff, student and agency.

PROBLEMS AND RISKS

Although the marginal or failing student in practicum is the focus of much debate (Brandon and Davies 1979, Bogo and Vayda 1987, Coleman, Collins and Aikins 1995), there is sparse research and information relating to at-risk students (Cole and Lewis 1993). Similarly, documentation regarding actual dismissal of students based on poor performance in the practicum has been minimal (Cole and Lewis 1993). Rosenblum and Raphael (1987) state that serious problems do occur in the practicum for students. The current climate of restructuring, downsizing and retrenchment has resulted in tense work environments. Shifting locations for human services workers are the norm. It is therefore imperative to discuss and document ways in which students can be assisted through the difficulties and challenges they encounter, especially about marginalization and exclusion. Facilitating discussions about oppression and the changing nature of practice is critical so that field educators and students are attuned to current issues and can work together to minimize risk. Risk in this context refers to those students who are marginalized and oppressed by virtue of membership in a particular group deemed to be minority by the dominant society. Students from oppressed locations are at risk in the practicum because they are made to feel inferior by the dominant society. These students fear backlash if they challenge discrimination and if they resist being subjugated by discriminatory behaviours.

The practicum is the place where significant issues pertaining to students' abilities and aptitudes for professional practice become evident. This course can therefore be referred to as the profession's "gatekeeper." It is often viewed as the most practical site for identifying performance difficulties which otherwise do not surface in the classroom or in completing academic assignments (Coleman et al. 1995). This "gatekeeping" function of the practicum is important for two reasons:

1. it signals the need to incorporate anti-oppression principles in field education when students with disabilities and other forms of oppression have to face major hurdles in their practicum;
2. it alerts field educators to students who have difficulties because of interpersonal problems and psychological or emotional issues.

Professional monitoring and assessment of student competence are evaluative components of the practicum. When there are problems, however, the ability to fully explore options is limited. For the field instructor, failing a student in the practicum is complicated and is not a common occurrence, due in part to the fear that students may resort to legal action:

> the literature argues that assessment of the practicum is difficult, of marginal performance especially so, and failure of the practicum is in practice rare. Moreover, it argues that the relationship between student and field educator is not simple or transparent and is influenced by several variables. (Eisenberg, Heycox and Hughes 1996: 34)

The following discussion highlights particular students at risk in the practicum and provides a context for examining and critically analyzing the roles of field educators, faculty and students. Socio-political issues as well as anti-oppression principles are crucial to this analysis.

THE RACIAL MINORITY STUDENT — *NOT EVEN BROKEN UP IN LITERATURE OF MY PLACEMENT*

- Let's not kill the goose that laid the golden egg.
- White middle class people are not being cared for.
- People with different religious beliefs ought to conform and respect existing standards.

The above excerpts were taken from my journal written almost a decade ago while I was a graduate student in placement at an educational institution with a white male field instructor who also held a prominent position within the community. These words, spoken by him, are tinged with racism and blatant and pernicious oppression. As a student, I had limited power to confront the supervisor, and I also knew that I could not rely on the university for support since these issues were not named in the academy. At both my placements I had to inform my supervisors about the realities of racial minority and immigrant people. Even in providing such information my identity and professionalism within white-dominant environments were never acknowledged, let alone open for dialogue. Faculty members were also ill-prepared to engage in these sensitive discussions. I felt I had to be the proponent of change: this has, in fact, been my reality throughout my university career (see Razack 2000).

Racism and oppression are embedded in our structures, institutions and the social fabric of society. People from racial minority groups have to face "everyday" forms of racism and discrimination (Essed 1990). The classroom can never be a totally safe place, nor can the agency/institution. The role of the field instructor is paramount in helping to facilitate the integration of theory and practice for students and in allowing the space for liberated discussions concerning professional identity (see Chapter Two). The topic of race, however, is always sensitive, and potentially volatile, to introduce in this dynamic. Marshack, Hendricks and Gladstein (1994) found that

> unless specifically asked to do so, few field instructors will identify issues of diversity in their educational assessments of students or explicitly refer to this data in describing a student's learning style ... field instructors tend to avoid addressing a student's potential learning needs or interests when these are influenced by issues of individual or interpersonal diversity. (78)

The field instructor sets the stage for the placement process: if discussions relating to identity and diversity are avoided, the racial minority student's learning and development as a professional are compromised. Jenkins (1981) observed that workers have a predilection for being accepting of differences but are unable to deal with the consequences. Gilborn (1996) states that "many teachers who are not 'prejudiced' in any conventional sense, nevertheless act in ways that have racist consequences" (172). A study of racial minority students in the practicum revealed that in-depth discussions of identity, subjugation, dominance and marginalization are not evident in discussions and teachings during the practicum (Razack 2001).

Social workers uphold the basic values of caring and empathy. These values are deeply entrenched within the profession. Caring and empathy, however, can lead to power and dominance when caring is craftily linked with control. Students tend to defer to the field instructor and hold this person as a model for practice. During field instruction seminars, field instructors at the school have shared their concerns about discussing issues of race and oppression with students, especially those with visible differences; they tend to adopt a "colour-blind" approach. According to Nebeker (1998),

> In strong contrast with educators' beliefs that "colorblind" policies promote acceptance and academic success for all students, research posits that students of color who are in school settings that

explicitly embrace cultural diversity hold a more positive school attachment than their cultural peers ... it is safe to assert that the adoption of the "race neutral" pedagogical and administrative practices does not benefit students ... "neutrality" only amounts to silencing of dissenting perspectives. (30)

Cooper and Lesser (1997) also state that an approach that ignores difference inhibits the practitioner's ability to question the client appropriately. This places constraints on the therapeutic relationship (333). This is also the reality in the minority student/majority field instructor relationship. It is incumbent on the field instructor to be knowledgeable about the implications of differences in the social work encounter. Students who engage in such discussions risk being labelled and marginalized in the practicum.

Students feel the burden to challenge racism and discrimination in their placement. Although many supervisors are caring and empathic, their responses to racism and oppression tend to be simplistic and superficial. In efforts to facilitate an antiracist and anti-oppressive structure, schools can develop a roster of minority field instructors who can be advisors to these students and to the school. It is not recommended that all racial minority students be matched with racial minority supervisors unquestioningly. However, choices must be available to both parties. Students need to be informed of the agency climate, mandate and policies, and the faculty advisor should have a keen knowledge of systemic inequalities. Field instructors need to challenge themselves to create a conceptual and practical knowledge base about racism and oppression in order to maximize the learning potential for all students. Faculty members need to be cognizant of how oppression is manifested in the practicum and be skilled to deal with challenges. Since the faculty member is the link between the university and the agency, she/he has to provide support and guidance, especially during tense situations.

EXAMINING THE PROCESS WITH STUDENTS WITH DISABILITIES

Over the course of my tenure I have worked with students with disabilities to plan, organize and implement the practicum. During each of these experiences I have felt outraged, disillusioned, disheartened and even powerless witnessing the systemic and structural barriers which persist for these students. Although there are advocacy groups and efforts to make the workplace more accessible, in reality, stigma, discrimination and labelling are still entrenched within the organizations. Systemic barriers are also effectively facilitated through the bodies of those in power when decisions are made about whether it is even feasible to interview a student with disabilities. Hearing the excuses and explanations can be frustrating: trying to maintain working relationships with the community and trying to avoid responding with a strong political voice for fear of legal reprisals can also sustain oppression.

According to Gregory (1996), disability is a relational term since it defines a person in relation to others based on an analysis of difference. For people with disabilities, this label marks their identity in terms of social interaction and location—they are defined by their disability and not by their strengths. The discourse on disability originated primarily from those who are able-bodied, and the emphasis has been on how the disability and deficiency lead to societal labelling. Mackelprang and Salsgiver (1996) state that social work has not embraced the causes of people with disability as it has other oppressed groups (312). The atrocities enacted on people with disabilities are extensive. Their origins are deeply embedded in a society whose belief systems include eugenics, shame and disgrace. The birth of disability consciousness arose in the 1960s when significant numbers of people with disability demanded access into mainstream society. Independent living centres emerged and the traditional medical paradigm was challenged. The work force has been included in this new consciousness, where lobbying and advocacy are used to persuade employers to hire people with disabilities. According to Basbaum (1995), our population is aging and therefore more people will likely incur disabilities. Medical technology allows a higher survival rate for people who suffer trauma, and many infants with significant impairments manage to stay alive. These trends suggest that services for people with disabilities are needed to ensure dignity, rights to justice and inclusion.

FIELD EDUCATION PERSPECTIVES

Field educators have responsibilities to provide all students with quality placements. Likewise professional accountability and responsibilities dictate that client service and educational standards not be compromised (Bial and Lynn 1995). As noted earlier, (Chapter Four), since agencies and universities have different concerns regarding education and practice, tensions can arise on both sides in seeking to redress some of these debilitating oppressive forces. Bial and Lynn (1995) state that tensions may emerge for students with disabilities at three points: negotiating and securing the placement and agency commitment; students' entry into the placement; and emergence of performance problems apparently caused by the disability (439). Agencies with specific mandates to work with people with disabilities are more open to offering placements to students with disability. Often the student with disability enters the program after having been a client of one of these programs or through their employment in the system. Since these students usually want to have a "mainstream" placement to be able to challenge themselves in different ways, they should be granted these opportunities. However, few agencies welcome students with disabilities.

The field coordinator also experiences tensions trying to fulfill the goals of the student. Professional values, legislation and student advocacy help to shape responses which will support the student in settings which could potentially be hostile and oppressive. Bargaining with agencies consists of cajoling, insisting, pressuring and subtly referring to anti-oppressive principles. Fears and stereotypes abound in the workplace: barriers to accessible practice also influence students' decisions not to disclose the disability. Students are reluctant to share some of the realities of their disability for fear of limiting their opportunities. Alternatively the mainstream providers face many dilemmas when these students knock on their door. I have respected students' decisions about self-disclosure and spent countless hours responding to their needs in recruiting agencies. Both scenarios about self-disclosure have been met with hostility, anger, questions and confusion by the field instructor and agency. Field instructors state that having advance information about a student's disability would not affect their decisions or their ability to honestly assess students' needs in the workplace. On the other hand, students and field administrators express the need for caution in providing information to the agency. Sadly both scenarios have produced negative responses which have been masked with benevolence and kindness, indicating that the climate is still oppressive and prejudiced for students with disabilities.

A VIEW TO CHANGE

Students with disability face tremendous hurdles in all aspects of the practicum. Negotiating and securing a practicum create stress and tensions especially if the student wants to work in a mainstream setting. Students need to be realistic about their capabilities and knowledgeable about oppression and marginalization to battle the rejections and discrimination they face in every stage of the process. Advocacy is crucial if more agencies are to become accessible for placements. Practitioners who work with people with disability need education and sensitive support. Employment for this particular population is abysmally low, and many are underemployed. Field instructors need to be experienced and supportive of the student with disability, and the agency should extend itself in promoting and valuing their work. The supervisors' patience and non-judgmental abilities are critical in planning and organizing the work, as well as during supervision and evaluation. Educating and sensitizing the staff at the workplace is also critical to effect a positive work space for all students. The university administration also plays a significant role in ensuring that the student and field instructor receive support and validation. Issues about disability deserve further study, especially in a climate where oppressions intersect and diverse realities emerge to produce a very different and unique professional climate.

THE SEXUAL MINORITY STUDENT

[handwritten note: MOST WORK AT JA/DV CENTRE HETEROSEXUAL]

Social work is not immune to the dominant ideology that infers that heterosexuality is the norm; therefore, those who do not identify themselves with this orientation are labelled as deviants and suffer the brutality of homophobia. Students who are from sexual minority groups face insidious and often silent forms of discrimination. By "silent," I refer to the ways in which gay, lesbian and bisexual students have to submerge their identity to "fit" into the mainstream in order to survive. These forms of oppression can wreak havoc on identity and professionalism. I referred earlier to interlocking oppression: we must be cognizant of the intersections of race, class, gender, age and ability when considering our shifting and multiple identities and experiences. Lorde (1990) has defined these intersections:

[handwritten note: THINK SITUATION AT SA/DV]

> Differences between ourselves as Black women are also being misnamed and used to separate us from one another. As a Black lesbian feminist comfortable with the many different ingredients of my identity, and a woman committed to racial and sexual freedom from oppression, I find I am constantly being encouraged to pluck out some one aspect of myself and present that as the meaningful whole, eclipsing or denying the other parts of myself. But this is a destructive and fragmenting way to live. (285)

Logan and Kershaw (1994) discuss the dominant ideology of the social work profession which stigmatizes and marginalizes those who do not fit normative standards. They outline historical language and legislation which has denied equal access and other considerations of their reality to those who suffer discrimination.

ENTERING THE FIELD OF PRACTICE

Heterosexism is an integral component to be addressed and integrated within the curriculum. Students who are taught from a structural, radical or feminist approach often challenge various forms of oppression. Confronting homophobia in the placement setting, however, poses risk—a sexual minority student can face damaging consequences. There are few articles which analyze the experiences of sexual minority students in the practicum. Messenger and Topal (1997) speak of their struggles and oppression during their field placement. Although both these students were "out" with family, friends and colleagues, they chose to identify themselves with their field instructor at different points in the practicum. They state that there were no clear procedures from the school to guide them and that they were acutely aware of their evaluation procedures and future career opportunities. Often there are no guidelines or policies at the workplace, or, when they do exist, they are not readily effected. Like the student with a disability, the sexual minority student may have already worked in many gay-positive environments and wants the challenge of mainstream work. This so-called challenge is, I believe, a professional trap for minority students since it provides another arena in which to promote dominant ideology. The minority student's presence may only fleetingly disturb or unsettle the agency context. Otherwise the business of practice is maintained from dominant Euro-Western traditions. As I did, these students have a desire to fit in, while, at the same time, challenging the norm and advocating for a particular population. Responding to this seduction can lead to damaging consequences since it could result in further disillusionment about the profession.[1]

Messenger and Topal (1997) did not disclose their sexual orientation to the staff for fear of being stigmatized and victimized. They were also advised against disclosing their sexual identities with their clients. However, they soon realized how much their personal lives were rooted within the professional context. They discovered that their field instructors were not equipped to handle their questions and struggles about self identification with clients, and there was no formal policy within the agency. Faculty can be supportive to the student but may not provide meaningful intervention if they do not have a conceptual and personal knowledge base of heterosexism. The field office may not have the experience to advise students about sensitive issues.

Structural changes are needed within the agency and university. Policies should include hiring sexual minority staff, in-service training for all, having antidiscriminatory policies and developing a library and resources (Messenger and Topal 1997). The school also needs to develop policies and guidelines about homophobia and clearly outline procedures when problems emerge for the student and field instructor. The field office staff needs to promote a positive space for sexual minority students to identify and seek support in their placements. At my university a task force was struck to research ways to promote a safe environment for sexual minority faculty, students and staff. In order to fulfill some of their recommendations, ongoing workshops have been provided for faculty and staff to meet and discuss ways in which a personal, professional and structural approach to change can be achieved. At these optional workshops we are provided with materials and a positive-space sticker for our office door so students are aware of a "safer" space to discuss issues. In the practicum it is also helpful for sexual minority faculty to assist in liaison with agencies. Generic policies and guidelines alone are not sufficient to promote change: we must ensure that all aspect of the field, seminars, field instruction, planning and orientation respond to the needs of sexual minority students and clients.

THE MATURE STUDENT

Mature learners return to university for a variety of reasons. They may have years of human services-related experience but seek further qualifications. Some of them are now embarking on a career after caring for children, while others may wish to upgrade or change their profession. Risk factors for mature students in the practicum include

- fear of failure,
- apprehension and feelings of incompetence about practice,
- the expectation that they should be more knowledgeable simply because they have been around longer (Bogo and Vayda 1987),
- juggling home and school responsibilities,
- minimizing their practicum learning because of prior experience,
- the age differential between supervisor and student,
- resistance to being a student,
- feeling equally or more competent than the field instructor (ibid.).

In Chapter Five I explained the power dynamics inherent in the field instructor/student relationship and how power operates in this process. Students also need to reflect on how they themselves can operate from oppressive locations in the practicum. Given the list of risk indicators stated above, it is helpful to note how some problematic behaviours can emerge for students in their relationship with the field instructor and in the placement. Some students can become particularly demanding of the field instructor and an air of superiority may emerge when there is a feeling that the mature student has more work experience. Likewise, field instructors may be particularly demanding and place high expectations on mature students.

Some students can be particularly demanding of the field educator. Others may minimize their experiences simply to complete the necessary hours for the practicum course, never fully challenging themselves. Students with experience in settings that have rigid guidelines and fairly entrenched and conservative practices may challenge the organization and field educator. All of these situations can create risk for students in the practicum. Therefore it is helpful for field educators to understand these changing dynamics in people's lives and assist such students to learn and practice advocacy, social action and antidiscriminatory practice approaches.

The field educator needs to understand the various dilemmas that a mature student may experience while in the practicum. The transition to the student role can be difficult, especially when there is a loss of income, status and power (Marshack 1991). The field educator needs to be cognizant of these situations and facilitate an openness to discussing role transitions. Significant differences in age between student and field educator may produce discomfort and tensions if, at the outset, these realities are not addressed. Many of these students face conflicting demands at home and feel guilty about going back to school. Power and authority conflicts can arise if the older student finds it difficult to accept direction. The student may also feel devalued if their employment and life experiences are not recognized.

SOME REFLECTIONS FOR CHANGE

The field educator can play a critical role in assisting the older student through some of these difficult situations. Recognition of the strengths and competencies mature students bring to the placement is important from the outset. Many are highly motivated to succeed and are focused on learning and challenging themselves. Their life experiences make them more resilient to workplace demands: they can be more self-reliant and capable in the changing work environment. The field educator should read the mature student's résumé prior to the pre-practicum interview in order to acknowledge the student's skills and experiences during the interview. The field educator needs to be knowledgeable of different learning styles which may be used by particular students. Given age differences, the field educator may opt to facilitate a climate of openness and collaboration so that the older student feels recognized and included. However, it may be necessary to guard against encouraging a collegial relationship where the student can become too self-reliant or passive about the practicum.

The older student, in collaboration with the field supervisor, needs to establish a learning contract and make connections between previously acquired knowledge and new learning. The university needs to caution the mature learner to accept the student role and not vie for equal status with the other employees or human services workers. Power issues are a factor in the field educator–student relationship, which may become more emphasized when the student is older, mature and experienced. Mature students may also hold deeply entrenched, narrowly focused ideas that make it difficult for them to work from different perspectives. For some, "unlearning" can be challenging and difficult.

It is imperative that the university provides learning opportunities for field educators to recognize these different dynamics and to successfully manage different learning styles. If mature students are unsuccessful in recognizing and dealing with initial fears and anxieties or, if they are too independent and authoritative, their status in the practicum moves from at-risk to conflictual and marginal. The field educator needs to facilitate ongoing dialogue with the student and maintain links with the university. Initial fears must be understood, acknowledged and shared by field educator and student. If the field educator feels intimidated, the student will sense the discomfort. In the event of difficulty in the practicum, meetings are necessary to assess the suitability of the environment for the student and to facilitate ways in which individual differences can be resolved.

PSYCHOLOGICAL AND EMOTIONAL DIFFICULTIES

Although our profession is deeply concerned with validating the emotional reactions of clients, we have been less comfortable addressing the emotional reactions of workers and students. (Grossman et al. 1991: 205)

Many students enter the human services field because they have had significant life experiences that have allowed them to go through a process of growth and change. Such experiences can relate to separation, divorce, physical and sexual violence and various forms of loss. These situations may have resulted in professional intervention where the student felt the impact of the therapeutic process. Often the student, as client, enters the profession hoping to become like their therapist, or they feel compelled to assist others in similar predicaments. Students do not freely share their past experiences as clients since they fear being labelled and stigmatized. It is primarily when the student is in difficulty that past history is shared. Indicators of problems are observed through inappropriate behaviours and questionable performance. Supervisors need to be trained to manage psychological and emotional difficulties as they emerge with practicum students.

Eisenberg, Heycox and Hughes (1996) discuss the relationship between field instructor and student in the practicum as a critical learning tool since the centrality of social work practice is the client–worker relationship. It is primarily through the relationship between client and field instructor that issues relating to the "personal" can be discussed. Since students' personal characteristics and emotional behaviours are not open to scrutiny, worker subjectivity needs to be considered as an educational issue (Grossman, Levine-Jordano and Shearer 1991). Reactions to clients, situations and other workers are based on our assumptions, biases, knowledge, personalities, skills and the influences of past events. Students therefore may overidentify with certain clients or become attached to a particular social issue. Traumatic situations in the practicum can also trigger past emotional issues for students. The field educator should be attuned to potential emotional risks as they emerge for students in the practicum, and should assist students through these difficult situations.

Grossman et al. (1991) suggest a five-stage framework to work through emotional difficulties. First, the engagement and orientation phase signifies the beginning of the field educator/student relationship where first impressions are formed and strengths and vulnerabilities are observed. These first impressions should be noted in order to make the acceptance decision and to consider further areas of development for the student. The second stage includes an assessment of students' vulnerabilities to countertransference in their work; at this time the field educator can allow students to discuss feelings and reactions to the assigned tasks. A female student with a history of abuse, working with male perpetrators, may have emotional conflicts. Likewise working with AIDS patients may engender fears of one's own mortality. Field educators can also share some of their initial fears in their practicum to assist the student through emotional difficulties. The third stage involves the area of planning and formulating a contract for work. Students may also plan cases and projects in areas where they may be more vulnerable, prone to emotional entanglements and in need of assistance. In the fourth stage of implementation, field educators can help students to handle emotional reactions by discussing coping strategies. During the termination phase and also during evaluation and supervision, the field supervisor can gently point out situations where the student was able to manage emotional difficulties effectively.

Students who wish to reveal sensitive information to their field supervisor need to be advised on appropriate self-disclosure procedures. Reeser and Wertkin (1997) conducted a study with students, field instructors and faculty liaisons about sharing sensitive student information and found that the majority of students were opposed to sharing such information with the field instructor. Rosenblum and Raphael (1983) suggest that a balance should be sought between students' rights to privacy and field instructors' rights to information. Others argue that sensitive information be minimally shared with the field instructor because of bias and future risks when seeking employment (Royse, Dhooper and Rompf 1993). Students ought not to be judged and analyzed because of a history of psychiatric and/or emotional issues.

The field instructor needs to be sensitive to students' emotional and psychological issues. If sensitive information is shared, the field instructor needs to listen empathically and seek ways to ensure that the student does not feel further victimized and/or labelled. Students should not have to terminate a placement unless their emotions interfere with their judgements and ability to function appropriately at the setting. If possible, alternative work duties can be assigned: if the student is still unable to perform adequately, then meetings between the faculty liaison, the student and the field instructor are mandatory.

SUMMARY

Several issues may emerge during the practicum which can cause risk for students. Challenges and difficulties arise for a variety of reasons, including changing socio-political terrains and economic factors. The practicum offers the students the opportunity to test knowledge and skills gained through academic courses together with life experiences. For those students who are marginalized through societal inequities the practicum can be dangerous and their learning can be compromised. Particular factors apply to older students: these need to be understood by the field educator as well as by the students themselves. For students with disabilities and from sexual minority groups together with others who have faced significant trauma and have overcome personal problems, the practicum can trigger difficulties.

Field education should comprise ongoing education, guidelines and policies to assist those students who face challenges by virtue of their designation as a member of a minority group. Likewise, agencies and field instructors need to engage in ongoing educational seminars in order to discuss stress-related factors. Faculty liaisons also play a critical role in these situations and should be informed and educated about the needs of students who face risk in the practicum. Anti-oppression principles need to be incorporated, as well as ways to understand how life experiences, marginality and resistance affect students' ability to fulfill the course expectations.

NOTE

1. Here I am suggesting that minority students are seduced to enter mainstream space because they want to be legitimized within the profession. These students often fear that their skills gained from working in ethno-specific and other minority settings will not be viewed positively when they seek employment. These concerns cause them to want to move from the margins/periphery to the centre. However, there can be danger in falling prey to this situation. When minority students enter mainstream space, they inevitably witness how oppressive mainstrream practice is and can feel further marginalized. They may also put themselves at risk if they voice their concerns regarding oppression and racism in the workplace. At times marginal change may occur when the agency encourages the minority student to plan and organize seminars about oppression. The burden falls on the minority student in most situations and, therefore, they continue to be labelled and can feel delegitimized in dominant settings. On the other hand, the student's identity can be ignored, causing further marginalization and internalization of oppression within the student.

Chapter Eight

North–South Collaborations: A Critical Examination of International Student Exchanges[1]

> The idea that promoting international exchanges in social work requires little more than an adventurous spirit, a willingness to endure discomforts, and a large dose of good intentions is widespread but naive and is likely to result in frequent cultural misunderstandings. (Midgley 1992: 21)

This final chapter focuses on a critical examination of international field placements. An examination of this topic expands the political dialogue of field education and suggests the need for a major research project. International exchanges are gaining attention in schools of social work, primarily in the area of the practicum. This proliferation of exchange opportunities has arisen out of demands from individual students and a desire from faculty to engage in international activity. There may also be some thought of internationalizing the curriculum, as a response to global and transnational contexts for practice. As a result of discussions with other educators about planning and organizing such placements and from engaging in such international placement activity in my own school, it became apparent to me that pedagogical and practice implications have not been sufficiently explored or integrated into the curriculum. Although individual benefits occur for students, there needs to be more focus on ways in which these international placement exchanges can enhance curriculum and practice in social work education.

This chapter examines the purpose, planning and nature of international exchanges, with particular emphasis on the perils and merits of exchanges. The discussion includes a critical analysis of the process and delivery of placement exchanges, as well as the implications. The notions of "professional imperialism" and transnational collaborations will be highlighted. This study, which includes observations and informal discussions both with students who have completed their placements abroad and with a few of the host advisors, begins a broader study into professional exchanges. Cultural differences, ethnicity, race and social location are important areas for consideration.

BACKGROUND TO THE RESEARCH

Over the past four years I have organized, facilitated and supervised international student placements. During the course of such exchanges questions were emerging for me as an educator committed to anti-oppressive pedagogy and practice issues (Razack 1999). Some of these questions are the following: Which students are applying for international placement and to what countries? What are the reasons behind their choices? Are there flows of students coming from the south and other "developing" countries and, if not, what are the implications of that? Is there a continued form of "professional imperialism" underlying such exchanges? What are the benefits to be gained by facilitating such exchanges? Some of these questions will be considered further in this analysis.

Students have discussed their experiences of culture shock and dissonance upon their return from international placement as well as the knowledge gained from experiencing a different cultural environment. While these experiences can in fact allow for new and shifting contexts for practice, deeper inquiry into our complicity in maintaining our privileged locations in the North are not usually emphasized. This area of social work deserves further research in order to promote anti-oppressive and anti-imperialist principles in international social work. To provide a context for the analysis, I begin with a brief outline of the history of international social work and placement exchanges.

INTERNATIONAL SOCIAL WORK EDUCATION

Social work can be viewed as an international profession simply because it is taught and practised in most "developing" and "developed" countries. The Western British influence has pervaded social work in "developing" countries: indigenous practices and theories are not given sufficient attention (Midgley 1990). More recent debates focus on the benevolent caring role of social workers in attempting to provide leadership and programs to other countries and the "benevolent imperialism" which could result especially through professional exchanges (Martinez-Brawley 1999). International exchanges, involving efforts to learn and glean from the "other," may be seen as colonizing activity. According to Spivak (1993), a form of "pretentious internationalism" in the West pervades academia as we attempt to respond to world realities.

Modern social work was constructed during World War II with aid in the settlement of displaced refugees, and the profession has since demonstrated a long-standing commitment to social justice issues and world peace (Estes 1992, Midgley 1990). Social workers continue to involve themselves in international service organizations and social welfare activities. Journals, such as *International Social Work,* and international associations, such as the International Federation of Social Welfare (IFSW) and the International Association of Schools of Social Work (IASSW) all attest to the international commitment of the profession. A small number of texts and conferences promote internationalism. However, the promotion of international goodwill and promise, the inclusion of internationalism in the curriculum, the gains from international exchanges, and the profound commitment to global justice which underlie such activities are not fully valued and integrated into pedagogy and practice (Healy 1988).

Johnson (1996) notes the more common ways in which international social work tends to be included in the curriculum: through elective courses; through integrating international material across courses; through providing some international field placements; through enrolling students from other countries; and through student, practitioner and faculty exchanges (189). In the global and transnational age, social work needs to be attached to international activities, such as those related to social welfare, population, immigration, urbanization, family reunification, poverty, HIV/AIDS, homelessness, the environment, health issues, inequalities and social injustices, violence, and socio-political and economic abuses (Estes 1992).

Many of our social problems are rooted in international dynamics which transcend local and cultural boundaries. It is imperative to critically analyze how international social work is being undertaken with a quiet hegemonic and imperialistic agenda. We need to focus on countering hegemonic structures and alliances among nations, which have resulted from increased trade, travel, flows of information, global economy, technological advancements and refugee resettlements (Hokenstad, Khinduka and Midgley 1992, Healy 1988, Healy 1986, Sanders 1977). Eaton (1973) exhorts professionals to broaden their perspectives in order to counteract local prejudices, to include a world-wide perspective and to learn intergroup relational skills (57–58).

Healy (2001) states that although social work is a recognized international profession and is practised in unique ways all over the world, the theoretical foundations of international approaches have not been seriously integrated into the curriculum. She reports that social work has not adopted or implemented an international perspective. More recent research indicates that there is content on internationalism but only in additive frames (Midgley 1997, Healy 1995). Adding special courses and some content in other courses results in a lack of integration or consideration of national issues. There is no solid conceptual framework for incorporating a global perspective on social issues (Asamoah, Healy and Mayadas 1997). As borders become more permeable through technology and within a global market economy and with constant movement of peoples across the globe, cross-cultural understandings from international perspectives are crucial in our work. Social issues know no boundaries, and global interdependence is relevant to social problem analysis.

Midgley's (1990) work focuses on the way in which social work emerged in many "Third World" countries through the influences of colonialism in social work practice and the replication of social service systems to resemble those in large metropolitan areas (296). Midgley (1997) describes how exchanges were welcomed between industrialized and developing nations initially, but, with increasing independence in formerly colonized countries, these unilateral exchanges are being questioned. Many of these "developing" countries are struggling to create indigenous practices after being overwhelmed with Western, British and colonial knowledge. As might be expected, traces of colonialism and imperialism linger because the flow of information about practice and teaching is unidirectional, coming from industrial to "developing" nations. This dilemma is not unique to developing countries—even in large metropolitan cities where there is diversity, post-colonialism is inherent in our teachings and practices. Our language, theories and knowledge are steeped in Eurocentrism, which continues to dominate our classrooms. It is crucial therefore to examine, analyze and critique international exchanges. Examining the flows of such exchanges and links is our ethical responsibility, as we are heavily involved and implicated through globalization, transnationalism and internationalization. We need to facilitate the required awareness and critical knowledge to continuously assess how dominance is produced and organized.

Internationalism is rooted in colonialism and imperialism: this is especially clear when we consider that the production of knowledge and other academic gains flow from North to South. Hegemony is therefore inherent in our pedagogy, practice, education and our attempts at globalization (Midgley 1997, Nimmagadda and Cowger 1999). We in the North ought to recognize interdependence in our work and seek ways to avoid taking a superior position. We continue to study and learn about the "other" with little attention to how these structural power relations sustain cultural and economic privilege. According to Fellows and S. Razack (1997), one's privilege is always dependent on the subordination of another.

International Exchanges

In the early seventies Eaton (1973) discussed the "international dimension" in social work education. He began with some observations and questions surrounding the nature of international exchanges. He noted the expense involved in such exchanges and wondered about the need to seek foreign troubles when many students did not realize the depth of social problems occurring "at home." He used such terms such as "luxury" and a "profligate waste" to describe exchanges. He also acknowledged the potential merit of exchanges and described the need for interdependence in areas such as welfare, health and other human service areas. Noting that social workers then (and likely still today) were middle-class women, he believed that exchanges could broaden perspectives and enhance motivation, education and research (57).

Cowan and Turner (1975) developed an international exchange where students were involved in an innovative community program. Students had to orient themselves to the host culture but did not refer to this phenomenon as culture shock because of being located within a similar Western/British context. The students referred to their role as "cultural ambassadors" and appreciated their growth experiences. Some benefits were realized by the school, since students shared their experiences didactically, and there was some reciprocity. Cowan and Turner (1975) noted the limitations of international exchanges in terms of cost and the need to visit the site. Horncastle (1996) examined an exchange program funded through the European Union ERASMUS funds. Although there were language differences, the dominant white context remained. While he recognized the benefits listed above, his focus was on the social, professional and personal gains for the students. He also recommended some changes, especially administrative ones. Some more recent exchanges have involved groups of students and faculty members who plan and organize exchanges to "developing" countries and then talk about their experiences, highlighting the administrative details of planning and organizing (CSWE 1999). A group exchange approach is the premise of a collaborative research project being conducted with schools of social work in Canada and Europe, with funds from the European Union.

Midgley (1997) discusses the multifaceted nature of international exchanges. He notes that exchanges involve collaborative efforts to discuss mutual concerns, provide reciprocity and can be unilateral where it is accepted that one party has expertise to share (177). He emphasizes the problems which could result if this expertise has not been requested and recommends a critical attitude towards international exchanges. Undoubtedly more recent critiques concerning the hegemony inherent in exchanges demand different forms of inquiry. This analysis critically focuses on such exchanges, not only through looking at attitudes toward them, but also examining the ways in which dominant theory and hegemonic structures are maintained.

Schools of social work across Canada have been focusing more attention on international field placements. There does not appear to be an infrastructure of support for negotiating and effecting international placements. Rather there are ad hoc efforts to place students in "foreign" countries and to reap the benefits through exchange visits and the promotion of international activity within universities. Students and faculty have discussed reactions to their visits, which range from culture shock and dissonance to cross-cultural understandings and an appreciation of practices in different cultures. While these experiences can contribute to new contexts for practice, deeper inquiry into our complicity in maintaining our privileged locations in the North is not usually emphasized. The process does not include a critique of our continued benevolent imperialist efforts as we utilize the experience of others to promote our own cross-cultural awareness. In the quotation at the beginning of this chapter, Midgley (1992) talks about individual goodwill and good intentions in doing international social work. However, individual goodwill and desire to understand and learn about the other rarely allow for understanding the historical imperial legacies of the profession and our role in sustaining dominant ideological forms. International placement exchanges, therefore, need further examination, since there is not a large, critical body of work in this area.

CRITICAL OVERVIEW OF INTERNATIONAL PLACEMENT EXCHANGES

Over the past five years I have negotiated and supervised fourteen international placements. The locations include India (two placements), Columbia, Barbados, Trinidad (two placements), Zimbabwe (three placements),

Australia, Sweden, Bahamas and California and Michigan, U.S.A. We have only hosted placement exchange students from Sweden. Since only two of our exchange students were second generation students from the host country, most had different racial, ethnic and cultural backgrounds from their host country. There was no financial assistance from the institution except for the first two students, who were able to secure course payment exemption. Some had to provide remuneration to the university and there were various arrangements in terms of supervision, accommodation and linkages.

All of the students reported disorientation and anxiety at the onset. Some were frustrated with the lack of arrangements and follow-up with the host university. While some of their frustrations were valid, the students needed to take time for orientation to the community and settling into their new surroundings. Some students expected to be placed immediately upon arrival and were impatient with the slowness of the process. It was also interesting that, while one student would take these difficulties with lack of arrangement in stride, another would denounce the placement immediately for its lack of professionalism and allege that the site should not be utilized as an international exchange in the future. It is important to note that arranging placements can be more viable in "developed" countries, because of access to technology. Connecting and creating a swift process is not easily managed in "developing" countries where the pace is slower and access to technology, resources and material is fairly limited. Frustrations often arise as a result of western thinking and approaches about organization and accountability. These issues need to be clarified with students who might try to impose western standards on different soil. Students must be very sensitive to issues of domination and power differential. In discussions with a broad section of students who completed their practicum abroad, it became apparent that White students benefit more than students of colour by virtue of their skin colour, which denotes more privilege, power and wealth to those in "developing" countries. White students overwhelmingly reported how they were constantly approached for favours.

Some host supervisors observed that the students who come with a keen awareness of racism and privilege still need to take time to struggle with re-orienting their personal and professional identity. Students need to recognize the shift in their identities as they are located within historical legacies of colonization in many of these countries. Some supervisors expressed concern about students who try to import a North American value base wholesale to the field. The student may need the space to critically analyze values, principles and ethical norms derived from the home context. Sensitivity is needed in the approach to learning from international locations and in the approach to theorizing from the knowledge gained to produce new meanings for practice.

All students, even those with initial difficulties and language differences, reported that their placements were innovative and challenging. Some of these students became very integrated in the research and development teams. Students reported being overwhelmed with some of the projects which had policy and political implications, yet they felt challenged and academically enriched from their experience. Many of the students observed the rigour of academic programs in "developing" countries and the extent of the field involvement. They learned about the culture, policy, practice and community development. Electronic mail helped to provide communication links with the students, and reports from supervisors have been overwhelmingly positive. One supervisor noted that transferability of skills should be crucial to this process and that we should seek to integrate this knowledge into curriculum and practice.

Historically, the practicum course is described by students as a valuable learning experience even when there are serious issues about racism and oppression (Razack 2001). Similarly all international students report benefits even when language and cultural barriers preclude full involvement and participation. These benefits, however, need to be critically analyzed in terms of imperialism, socio-economic privilege, benevolence and paternalism.

ENGAGED FLUID PERSPECTIVES

There are no theories or guidelines for international student exchanges. As stated earlier, one author questioned the need for exchanges at all, when local problems abound. There is ample evidence of the benefits of international placements, although many cautionary notes should be figured into the design, approach and implementation. The language is critical. Why do we refer to these placements as exchanges when they occur by and large on a unidirectional scale, from Western to "developing" countries? What efforts are currently underway to shift the pendulum in order to capture and reap the benefits of true exchange? Are we sustaining our parochial habits and cultural hegemony through these exchanges? In a discussion with one host supervisor she clearly noted the challenge and learning which accrued for her through supervising a student. We have not yet theorized and produced a knowledge base to incorporate such benefits into the curriculum, pedagogy and practice.

According to Taylor (1999), social work is a contextual profession and varies considerably according to the cultural context within which it operates (330). Some fundamental values, however, apply across boundaries and are of relevance internationally. This core of knowledge includes "education for social policy development, team-building, networking, conflict resolution and organizational development ... self-help and mutual aid and the use of informal and indigenous helping networks is essential" (Taylor 1999: 317). Students seeking international placements need to have a strong hold on the theoretical and practice implications for international social work. This knowledge base should include understandings of social issues from the host perspectives, which must be predicated on an understanding of imperialism, colonization, postcoloniality and transnational perspectives. Some schools provide preparatory courses for students to discuss issues such as culture shock, policy and cross-cultural counselling issues. Procedures utilized appear to be inconsistent and there are few attempts to continue a dialogue before, during and after these placement exchanges.

Nimmagadda and Cowger (1999) explore how Western theories become "indigenized" by local practitioners in "developing" contexts. They began by listing the difficulties encountered by practitioners in transferring Western ideology, knowledge and technology. These efforts often create conflict and confusion. The acceptance of a blind universalism without efforts to seek to put content and design into an indigenous context creates difficulties for worker and client. In other words "professional imperialism" continues when Western influences dominate developing local contexts. However, their findings instill hope that new theories will be effected to aid the "developed" countries and to decrease their power and stronghold on the theory building of the profession. Nimmagadda and Cowger (1999) state that:

> despite being taught foreign models of practice, practitioners appear to be quite creative in modifying such knowledge and making it more appropriate for the local culture. Those who might believe that social work practice knowledge might be destructive because of cultural incongruity give too much credit to the power of such knowledge and too little credit to the power of the local culture and the ingenuity of culturally grounded practitioners. (274–75)

Our social work students need to understand how to indigenize knowledge to suit their particular locations. This concept is fairly new for western social workers who come with the belief that their knowledge is supreme and relevant to any context. With basic understanding of power and privilege they assume they can then practice their art. However, when they are confronted with cultural, economic and social differences, the struggles emerge.

Whitmore and Wilson (1997) provide a conceptual framework to assist in examining the nature of partnerships and collaboration with "developing" agencies and countries. They begin by noting that development efforts through exchanges have not significantly altered the economic situation for the majority of people in the world. In fact, their situation has declined considerably. Therefore, the need to pay attention to the effectiveness of these international efforts is critical. We ought to question who continues to reap the major benefits from these exchanges. Although their analysis is based more on faculty research collaboration, there are some implications for international student exchange theory. "Accompanying" the process or "acompanamiento," contains a set of principles useful for collaborations in various contexts:

> These include non-intrusive collaboration, mutual trust and respect, a common analysis of what the problem is, a commitment to solidarity, equality in the relationship, an explicit focus on process and the importance of language. (58)

The authors suggest this approach include social work theory and practice and feminist principles together with structural and conjectural analyses. Structural analysis relates to understanding the larger economic, social and political structures which are oppressive to all peoples and pervade working relationships. Conjectural analysis focuses on the present situation and involves examining political issues at any point in the process and acting on them (57). Their approach assumes that the space to collaborate on an equal level has already been established. However, organizing the space is crucial for a commitment to solidarity and equality in the relationship. Their analysis, however, provides many useful steps in organizing a theoretical framework for professional exchanges. They highlight predeparture characteristics as including qualities such as:

> professional commitment, technical skills, relationship-building behaviours, personal confidence and initiative perseverance, flexibility and a desire to learn about other cultures, an ability to work in teams, a low need for material things or status, a high tolerance for ambiguity and self-discipline. (60)

Crucial to these principles, guidelines and theoretical approaches is the idea of reciprocity in the process. Who is responsible for shaping the benefits? How can the perils be discussed in a way in which there is respect, mutuality and shared experiences? In collaborations, whether North/South or East/West, there are particular areas to highlight (Razack 2000a). Whitmore and Wilson (1997) discuss North/South partnerships and note the need for a "critical structural analysis." Although their analysis includes examinations of dominance, subjugation, marginalization, economic strength, transnational structures, imperialism, colonization, race and racism, the contexts for discussing these historical legacies are not effectively and clearly stated as integral to the process. Rather they focused their efforts on the philanthropic need to maintain egalitarian principles to which they fought to adhere in their exchange. They also noted when their cultural and North American superiority crept into the process.

A critical knowledge base is required for effecting anti-imperialist international collaborations and exchanges. It is evident that students felt that they benefitted from the exchanges through their assigned tasks, cross-cultural alliances, and experiences of "differences" in terms of the ideology of professional theory and practice. The uneasiness however lies in hearing the reports of their experiences and observing the approaches to "doing" international social work. What I have observed is the avoidance of discussing social location, benevolence, witnessing and seeing the "other" through imperial eyes, and the lack of knowledge, ability and willingness to discuss how one's dominance is implicated in another's subordination. This is the space we need to create to engage in theorizing international social work. How this space is constructed to ensure this dialogue is critical to effective and ethical international social work practice.

CONCLUSION

International exchanges have become fashionable in schools of social work. While there are inherent benefits in such exchanges, relating to cross-cultural awareness and comparative analysis of social issues, we need to interrogate the unidirectional nature of these exchanges. When we question why the flow of exchanges *to* "developing'" countries is more prevalent, there is little discussion about the forces of imperialism, the legacies of colonization and the profound effect on identity and positioning of dominant or marginalized status. What I challenge in international placement considerations is the lack of space to discuss these issues and to build theories and a sustained critique of the process. There is little effort to share the inherent change processes which occur for the students and the benefits and burdens of the process. Other questions remain. What is the effect of our students on the host agency and university? How can we ensure that there is reciprocity and mutuality? Further study into these issues is needed for us to claim honest benefits in exchanges; otherwise we may be replicating hegemonic, imperialistic behaviours. The global concerns are at times overwhelming for students. Efforts towards change can begin from examining the forces that maintain this uneven distribution of goods and resources and that sustain the power of certain governments and transnational corporations. This study does not provide a prescriptive theoretical model. It alerts us to ways in which we should begin to question our agenda in international exchanges.

NOTE

1. This paper is adapted from an article published in *International Social Work*.

References

Abram, F., M.R. Hartung, and S.P. Wernet. 2000. "The non-M.S.W. task supervisor, M.S.W. field instructor, and the practicum student: A triad for high quality field education." *Journal of Teaching in Social Work* 20, 1-2.

Assamoah, Y., L. Healy, and N. Mayadas. 1997. "Ending the International-Domestic Dichotomy: New Approaches to a Global Curriculum for the Millennium." *Journal of Social Work Education* 3, 2 (Spring/Summer).

Aylward, C.A. 1999. *Canadian Critical Race Theory: Racism and the Law.* Halifax: Fernwood.

Aymer, C., and A. Bryan. 1996. "Black students' experience on social work courses: Accentuating the positives." *British Journal of Social Work* 26.

Barsky, A. 1995. "A student-centred approach to culturally diverse role play exercises." *Canadian Social Work Review* 12, 2.

Basbaum, M. 1995. "Programs for the physically disabled." In J.C. Turner and F. J. Turner (eds.), *Canadian Social Welfare.* Third Edition. Toronto: Allyn and Bacon.

Beecharan, A. and L. Burrell. 1994. "A rock and a hard place: Trying to provide culturally sensitive field experiences in rural, homogeneous communities." *Journal of Multicultural Social Work* 3, 1.

Behling, J., C. Curtis, and S. Foster. 1982. "Impact of sex role combinations on student performance in field instruction." *Journal of Education for Social Work* 18, 2.

Bell, L., and S. Webb. 1992. "The invisible art of teaching for practice: Social workers' perceptions of taking students on placement." *Social Work Education* 12, 3.

Bial, M.C., and M. Lynn. 1995. "Field education for students with disabilities: Front door/back door; negotiation/accommodation/mediation." In G. Rogers (ed.), *Field Education: Views and Visions.* Dubuque, IA: Kendall/Hunt.

Black, J., M. Maki, and J. Nunn. 1994. "Does Race Affect the Social Work Student–Field Instructor Relationship?" Paper presented at the Conference of Field Education, June, Calgary, Alberta.

Blommaert, J., and J. Verschueren. 1998. *Debating Diversity.* London: Routledge.

Bocage, M., E. Homonoff, and P. Riley. 1995. "Measuring the impact of the current state and national fiscal crises on human service agencies and social work training." *Social Work* 40.

Bogo, M., and E. Vayda. 1987. *The Practice of Field Instruction in Social*

Work: Theory and Process. Toronto: University of Toronto.

_____. 1998. *The Practice of Field Instruction in Social Work: Theory and Process.* Second Edition. Toronto: University of Toronto.

Bonilla-Silva, E. 2000. "This is a white country: The racial ideology of the western nations of the world-system." *Sociological Inquiry* 70, 2, 188–214.

Bracken, D., and C. Wamsley. 1992. "The Canadian Welfare State: Implications for the Continuing Education of Canadian Social Workers." *The Social Worker* 60, 1 (Spring).

Brah, Avtar. 1996. *Cartographies of diaspora: Contesting identities.* London: Routledge.

Brandon, J., and M. Davies. 1979. "The limits of competence in social work: The assessment of marginal students in social work education." *British Journal of Social Work* 9, 3.

Brown, L., and M. Root. 1990. *Diversity and Complexity of Feminist Therapy.* New York: Harrington Park Press.

Burgess, R., D. Crosshall, L. LaRose-Jones. 1992. *The Black Students' Voice.* London: ABPO/ABSW/CEETSW.

Canadian Association of Schools of Social Work (CASSW). 1991. "Social work education at the crossroads: The challenge of diversity." Report of the Task Force on Multicultural Issues in Social Work Education, Ottawa.

_____. 2000. Heritage Research Project.

Carillo, D., C. Holzhalb, and B. Thyer. 1993. "Assessing Social Work Students' Attitudes Related to Cultural Diversity: A Review of Selected Measures." *Journal of Social Work Education* 29, 3 (Fall).

Carniol, B. 2000. *Case Critical: Challenging Social Services in Canada.* Fourth Edition. Toronto: Between the Lines.

Carty, L. (ed.). 1993. *And Still We Rise: Feminist Political Mobilizing in Contemporary Canada.* Toronto: Women's Press.

Chambon, A., and A. Irving. 1998. "Introduction." In A. Chambon, A. Irving and L. Epstein (eds.). *Reading Foucault for Social Work.* New York: Columbia University Press.

Chambon, A., A. Irving and L. Epstein (eds.). 1998. *Reading Foucault for Social Work.* New York: Columbia University Press.

Chand, A., M. Doel and J. Yee. 1999. "Tracking social work students' understanding and application of antidiscriminatory practice." *Issues in Social Work Education* 19, 1.

Chau, K. 1991. "Social Work with Ethnic Minorities: Practice Issues and Potentials." *Journal of Multicultural Social Work* 1, 1.

Choy, B., A. Leung, T. Tam, and C. Chu. 1998. "Roles and tasks of field instructors as perceived by Chinese social work students." *Journal of Teaching in Social Work* 16, 2.

Christensen, C.P. 1992. "Training for cross-cultural social work with immigrants, refugees, and minorities: A course model." *Journal of Multicultural Social Work* 2, 1.

Christensen, C. 1995. "Immigrant Minorities in Canada." In J. Turner and F. Turner (eds.), *Canadian Social Welfare*. Scarborough, ON: Allyn and Bacon.

Cleak, H., L. Hawkins, and L. Hess. 2000. "Innovative field options." In L. Cooper and L. Briggs (eds.), *Fieldwork in the Human Services*. St. Leonards, Australia: Allen and Unwin.

Coady, N. 1995. "A reflective/inductive model of practice: Emphasizing theory-building for unique cases versus applying theory to practice." In G. Rogers (ed.), *Social Work Field Education: Views and Visions*. Dubuque, IA: Kendall/Hunt.

Cole, B., and Lewis, R. 1993. "Gatekeeping through termination of unsuitable social work students: Legal issues and guidelines." *Journal of Social Work Education* 29, 2.

Coleman, H., D. Collins, and D. Aikins. 1995. "The student at risk in the practicum." In G. Rogers (ed.), *Social Work Field Education: Views and Visions*. Dubuque, IA: Kendall/Hunt.

Conklin, J.J., and M.C. Borecki. 1991. "Field education units revisited: A model for the 1990s." In D. Schneck, B. Grossman, and U. Glassman (eds.), *Field Education in Social Work: Contemporary Issues and Trends*. Dubuque, IA: Kendall/Hunt.

Cooper, L. 1996. "Peer Learning in Field Education: Resources, Skills and Experiences." *Proceedings*. Joint Work Congress of the International Federation of Social Workers and the International Association of Schools of Social Work, Hong Kong. July.

_____. 2000. "Teaching and Learning in the Human Servces." In L. Cooper and L. Briggs.

Cooper, L., and L. Briggs, (eds.). 2000. *Fieldwork in the Human Services*. St. Leonards, Australia: Allen and Unwin.

Cooper, M., and J. Lesser. 1997. "How race affects the helping process: A case of therapy." *Clinical Social Work Journal* 25, 3.

Costoglou, Penny. 1996. *Summary Report of Cutbacks in Ontario*. Toronto: Ontario Social Development Council.

Council on Social Work Education (CSWE). 1999. International Symposia, San Francisco, March.

Cowan, B., and F. Turner. 1975. "Overseas field placement: An educational experiment." *Journal of Education for Social Work* 11, 2.

De Montigny, G. 1995. *Social Working: An Ethnography of Front Line Practice*. Toronto: University of Toronto Press.

Dei, G.J. 1996. *Theory and Antiracism Education*. Halifax: Fernwood.

Delgado, R. (ed.). 1995. *Critical Race Theory; The Cutting Edge*. Philadelphia: Temple University Press.

Dominelli, L. 1988. *Antiracist Social Work: A Challenge for White Practitioners and Educators*. Basingstoke, U.K.: Macmillan.

_____. 1991. "Race, Gender and Social Work." In M. Davies (ed.), *The Sociology of Social Work*. London, U.K.,: Routledge.

_____. 1996. "Deprofessionalizing Social Work: Anti-Oppressive Practice, Competencies and Postmodernism." *British Journal of Social Work* 26.

Donner, S. 1996. "Field Work Crisis: Dilemmas, Dangers and Opportunities." *Smith College Studies in Social Work* 66, 3, (June).

Eaton, J.W. 1973. "The international dimension in social work education." *International Social Work* 16, 2.

Edgerton, S.H. 1993. "Toni Morrison teaching the interminable." In C. McCarthy and W. Crichlow (eds.), *Race, Identity and Representation in Education*. New York: Routledge.

Eisenberg, M., K. Heycox, and L. Hughes. 1996. "Fear of the personal: Assessing students in practicum." *Australian Social Work* 49, 4.

Epstein, L. 1999. "The culture of social work." In A. Chambon, A. Irving and L. Epstein (eds.), *Reading Foucault for Social Work*. New York: Columbia University Press.

Essed, P. 1990. *Everyday Racism: Reports from Women of Two Cultures*. Almeda, CA: Hunter House.

Estes, R.J. 1992. *Internationalizing Social Work Education: A Guide for Resources for a New Century*. Philadelphia: University of Pennsylvania.

Fellows, M.L., and S. Razack. 1997. "The Race to Innocence: Confronting Hierarchical Relations among Women." *The Journal of Gender, Race and Justice* 1, 2.

Ferguson, S.A. 1996. "Towards an antiracist social service organization." *Journal of Multicultural Social Work* 4, 1.

Fleras, A., and J.L. Elliott. 1999. *Unequal Relations: An Introduction to Race, Ethnic, and Aboriginal Dynamics in Canada*. Third edition. Boston, MA: Prentice Hall/Allyn and Bacon.

Fook, J., M. Ryan, and L. Hawkins. 1997. "Towards a theory of social work expertise." *British Journal of Social Work* 27.

Fortune, A., and J. Abramson. 1993. "Predictors of satisfaction with field practicum among social work students." *Clinical Supervisor* 11, 1.

Foucault, M. 1980. *Power/Knowledge: Selected Interviews and Writings*. New York: Pantheon Books.

Frankenberg, R. 1993. *White Women, Race Matters: The Social Construction of Whiteness*. Minneapolis: University of Minnesota Press.

_____ (ed.). 1997. *Displacing Whiteness: Essays in Social and Cultural Criticism*. Durham, NC: Duke University Press.

Freire, P. 1970. *Pedagogy of the Oppressed*. New York: Continuum.

_____. 1990. "A critical understanding of social work. *Journal of Human Services* 1, 1.

Fusco, L.J. 1995. "Principles of practicum social work education." In G. Rogers (ed.), *Social Work Field Education: Views and Visions*. Dubuque: Kendall/Hunt.

Garcia, B., and M. Melendez. 1997 "Concepts and methods in teaching oppression courses." *Journal of Progressive Human Services* 8, 1.

Giddings, M.M., K.H. Thompson, and T.P. Holland. 1997. "The relationship between student assessments of agency work climate and satisfaction with the practicum." *Arete* 21, 2.

Gil, D.G. 1998. *Confronting Injustice and Oppression.* New York: Columbia University Press.

Gilborn, D. 1996. "Student roles and perspectives in antiracist education: A crisis of white ethnicity." *British Educational Research Journal* 22, 2.

Gold, N., and M. Bogo. 1992. "Social Work Research in a Multicultural Society: Challenges and Approaches." *Journal of Multicultural Social Work* 2, 4.

Goldstein, H. 1993. "Field Education for Reflective Practice: A Re-Constructive Proposal." *Journal of Teaching in Social Work* 18, 1/2.

Gonsales Del Valle, A., Merdinger, J., Wrenn, R., and D. Miller. 1991. "The field practicum and transcultural practice: An integrated model." *Journal of Multicultural Social Work* 1, 3.

Gordon, E.B. 1995. "Educating for Empowerment: Teaching Policy and Practice with Individuals with Disabilities." *Arete* 20, 1 (Spring).

Gould, N., and I. Taylor (eds.). 1996. *Reflective Learning for Social Work.* Aldershot: Arena.

Gray, M., C. van Rooyen, J. Gaha, and G. Rennie. 2000. "Social work political participation: A comparative study." Paper presented at the Joint Conference of the International Federation of Social Workers and the International Association of Schools of Social Work, Montreal, Canada, July.

Gregory, S. 1996. "The disabled self." In M. Wetherell (ed.), *Identities, Groups and Social Issues.* London: Sage.

Grossman, B., N. Levine-Jordano, and P. Shearer. 1991. "Working with students' emotional reactions in the field: An education framework." In D. Schneck, B. Grossman and U. Glassman (eds.), *Field Education in Social Work: Contemporary Issues and Trends.* Dubuque, IA: Kendall/Hunt.

Hagen, B.J.H. 1989. "The practicum instructor: A study of role expectations." In M.S. Raskin (ed.), *Empirical Studies in Field Education.* New York: Haworth Press.

Hall, S. 1996. "Introduction: Who needs identity?" In S. Hall and P. du Gay (eds.), *Questions of Cultural Identity.* London: Sage.

Harrison, D.W. 1987. "Reflective practice in social care." *Social Service Review* (September).

Haynes, A., and R. Singh. 1992. "Ethnic-Sensitive Social Work Practice: An Integrated, Ecological, and Psychodynamic Approach." *Journal of Multicultural Social Work* 2, 2.

Hawthorne, L., and Holtzman, R. 1991. "Directors of field education: Critical role and dilemmas." In D. Schneck, B.Grossman and U. Glassman (eds.), *Field Education in Social Work: Contemporary Issues and Trends.* Dubuque, IA: Kendall/Hunt

Healy, L. 1986. "The international dimension in social work education: Current efforts, future challenges." *International Social Work* 29, 2.

_____. 1988. "Curriculum building in international social work: Toward preparing professionals for the global age." *Journal of Social Work Education* 24, 3.

_____. 1995. "Comparative and international overview." In T.D. Watts, D. Elliott, and N. Mayadas (eds.), *International Handbook on Social Work Education*. Westport, CT: Greenwood.

_____. 2001. *International Social Work: Professional Action in an Interdependent World*. New York: Oxford.

Henry, F., C. Tator, W. Mattis, and T. Rees. 1995. *The Colour of Democracy*. Toronto: Harcourt Brace.

Hill-Collins, P. 1990. *Black Feminist Thought: Knowledge, Consciousness and the Politics of Empowerment*. Boston: Unwin Hyman.

Hokenstad, M.G., S.K. Khinduka and J. Midgley (eds.). 1992. *Profiles in International Social Work*. Washington, DC: NASW Press.

Horncastle, J. 1996. "The experience of social work students in foreign placements." In P. Ford and P. Hayes (eds.), *Educating for Social Work: Arguments for Optimism*. Aldershot: Avebury.

Hugman, R. 1996. "Professionalization in social work: The challenge of diversity." *International Social Work* 39, 2.

Insoo, K., and S. Miller. 1992. "Working with Asian American Clients: One Person at a Time." *Families in Society: The Journal of Contemporary Human Services* 356–63.

Irving, A. 1999. "Waiting for Foucault: Social work and the multitudinous truth(s) of life." In A. Chambon, A. Irving and L. Epstein (eds.), *Reading Foucault for Social Work*. New York: Columbia University Press.

Jarman-Rhode, L., J. McFall, P. Kolgar, and G. Strom. 1997. "The Changing Context of Social Work Practice: Implications and Recommendations for Social Work Education." *Journal of Social Work Education* 33, 1.

Jenkins, S. 1981. *The Ethnic Dilemma in Social Services*. New York: Free Press.

Johnson, W. 1996. "International activity in undergraduate social work education in the United States." *International Social Work* 39, 2.

Jordan, M. 1982. "Piggy in the middle: Social Work Education—A view from the field." In R. Bailey and P. Lee (eds.), *Theory and Practice in Social Work*. London: Blackwell.

Kadushin, A. 1976. *Supervision in Social Work*. New York: Columbia University Press.

_____. 1990. *Supervision in Social Work*. Third Edition. Columbia: Columbia University Press.

Kamerman, S.B. 1996. "The New Politics of Child and Family Policies." *Social Work* 41, 5.

Kilpatrick, A.C., and T.P. Holland. 1993. "Management of the field instruction program in social work education." *Journal of Teaching in Social Work* 7, 1.

Kolar, P., M. Patchner, W. Schutz and L. Patchner. 2000. Assessing the impact of managed care on field education in schools of social work. *Arete* 24, 2.

Kolb Morris, J. 1993. "Interacting Oppressions: Teaching Social Work Content on Women of Colour." *Journal of Social Work Education* 29, 1 (Winter).

Ladson-Billings, G. 1998. "Just what is critical race theory and what is it doing in a 'nice' field like education?" *International Journal of Qualitative Studies in Education,* 11.

Lloyd, L. 1998. "The post- and the anti-: Analysing change and changing analyses in social work." *British Journal of Social Work* 28.

Logan, J., and S. Kershaw. 1994. "Heterosexism and social work education: The invisible challenge. *Social Work Education* 13, 3.

Longres, J.F. 1991. "Towards a Status Model of Ethnic Sensitive Practice." *Journal of Multicultural Social Work* 1, 1.

Longres, J.F., and G.B. Seltzer. 1994. "Racism: Its implications for the education of minority social work students." *Journal of Multicultural Social Work* 3, 1.

Lorde, A. 1990. "Age, Race, Class, and Sex: Women Redefining Difference." In R. Ferguson, M. Gever, T. Minh-ha and C. West (eds.), *Out There: Marginalization and Contemporary Cultures.* New York: The New Museum of Contemporary Art.

Macey, M., and E. Moxon. 1996. "An Examination of Antiracist and Anti-Oppressive Theory and Practice in Social Work Education." *British Journal of Social Work* 26, 3.

Mackelprang, R.W., and R.O. Salsgiver. 1996. "People with disabilities and social work: Historical and contemporary issues." *Social Work: Journal of the National Association of Social Workers* 41, 1.

Marcoccio, K. 1995. "Identifying oppression in language: The power of words." *Canadian Social Work Review* 12, 2 (Summer).

Margolin, L. 1997. *Under the Cover of Kindness; The Invention of Social Work.* Charlottesville: University Press of Virginia.

Marshack, E. 1991. "The older student: Social work's new majority." In D. Schneck, B. Grossman, and U. Glassman (eds.), *Field Education in Social Work: Contemporary Issues and Trends.* Dubuque: IA: Kendall/Hunt.

Marshack, E., and U. Glassman. 1991. "Innovative models for field instruction: Departing from traditional methods." In D. Schneck, B. Grossman, and U. Glassman (eds.), *Field Education in Social Work: Contemporary Issues and Trends.* Dubuque: IA: Kendall/Hunt.

Marshack, E.F., C.O. Hendricks and M. Gladstein. 1994. "The commonality of difference: Teaching about diversity in field instruction." *Journal of Multicultural Social Work* 3, 1.

Martinez-Brawley, E. 1999. "Social work, postmodernism and higher education." *International Social Work* 42, 3.

Mawhiney, A.M. 1995. "The first nations in Canada." In J. Turner and F. Turner (eds.), *Canadian Social Welfare.* Third Edition. Scarborough, Ontario: Allyn and Bacon.

McCarthy, C., and W. Crichlow (eds.). 1993. *Race, Identity and Representation in Education.* New York: Routledge.

McChesny, M.L. 1999. "Agency-based social work field instruction orientation and training." *Dissertation Abstracts International,* A: The Humanities and Social Sciences. 60(2), Aug. 551.-A.

Messenger, L., and M. Topal. 1997. "'Are you married?' Two sexual-minority students: Perspectives on field placements." *Affilia* 12, 1.

Midgley, J. 1990. *International Social Work: Learning from the Third World.* Washington, DC: National Association of Social Workers Press.

_____. 1992. "The challenge of international social work." *Profiles in International Social Work.* Washington, DC: National Association of Social Workers Press.

_____. 1997. *Social Welfare in Global Context.* Thousand Oaks, CA: Sage Publications.

Midgley, J., and M. Livermore. 1996. "Promoting Social Development through Social Work Practice: Implications for Social Work Education." *Proceedings,* Joint Work Congress of the International Federation of Social Workers and the International Association of Schools of Social Work, Hong Kong, July.

Mishra, R. 1999. *Globalization and the Welfare State.* Cheltenham: Edward Elgar.

Moffattt, K. 1994. "Teaching Social Work Practice as a Reflective Process." Paper presented to the 27th Congress, The International Schools of Social Work, Amsterdam, July.

Mok, B.H. 1993. "Integrative seminar: A cognitive approach to linking theory and practice in social work." *International Social Work* 36.

Moore, D. 2000. "Managing Fieldwork." In L. Cooper, and L. Briggs (eds.), *Fieldwork in the Human Services.* St. Leonards, Australia: Allen and Unwin.

Morris, J. 1993. "Interacting oppressions: Teaching social work content on women of color." *Journal of Social Work Education* 29, 1.

Mullaly, B. 1997. *Structural Social Work: Ideology, Theory, and Practice.* Second Edition. Toronto: Oxford University Press.

Mullender, A. 1995. "The assessment of anti-oppressive practice in the Diploma in Social Work." *Issues in Social Work Education* 15, 1.

Nagar, R., and H. Leitmer. 1998. "Contesting social relations in communal places: Identity politics among Asian communities in Dar es Salaam." In R. Fincher and J. Jacobs (eds.), *Cities of Difference.* New York: Guilford Press.

Nebeker, K.G. 1998. "Critical race theory: A white graduate student's struggle with this growing area of scholarship." *Qualitative Studies in Education* 11, 1.

Nimmagadda, J., and C.D. Cowger. 1999. "Cross-cultural practice: Social worker ingenuity in the indigenization of practice knowledge." *International Social Work* 42, 3.

Norberg, W., and D. Schneck. 1991. "A dual matrix structure for field education." In D. Schneck, B. Grossman, and U. Glassman (eds.), *Field Education in Social Work: Contemporary Issues and Trends*. Dubuque, IA: Kendall/Hunt.

Ontario Federation of Labour (CLC). 1996. "The Common Sense Revolution: 449 Days of Destruction." *Fight Back Facts*. September 14.

Ontario Social Safety Network. 1996. *Ontario Welfare Rate Cuts: An Anniversary Report*. October.

Parton, N. 2000. "Some thoughts on the relationship between theory and practice in and to social work." *British Journal of Social Work* 30.

Pease, B., and J. Fook (eds.). 1999. *Transforming Social Work Practice: Postmodern Critical Perspectives*. London: Routledge

Perera, S., and J. Pugliese. 1997. "Racial Suicide: The Re-Licensing of Racism in Australia." *Race and Class* 39, 2.

Perry, P. 2001. "White means never having to say you're ethnic: White youth and the construction of 'cultureless' identities." *Journal of Contemporary Ethnography* 30, 1.

Pharr, S. 1988. *Homophobia: A Weapon of Sexism*. Oakland, CA: Chardon Press.

Potocky, M. 1997. "Multicultural social work in the United States: A review and critique." *International Social Work* 40.

Preston, L. 1999. "Organization and Management of the Process of Practicum: Review of student practicum evaluations." Practicum Task Force Committee, School of Social Work, York University, Fall.

Rabin, C., R. Savaya, and P. Frank. 1994. "A joint university–field agency: Toward the integration of classroom and practicum." *Journal of Social Work Education* 30, 1.

Raskin, M. 1982. "Factors associated with student satisfaction in undergraduate social work field placement." *Arete* 7, 1.

Razack, N. 1999a. "Antidiscriminatory Practice: Pedagogical Struggles and Challenges." *British Journal of Social Work* 29, 2.

_____. 1999b. "Anti-oppressive Social Work: A Model for Field Education." In Gwat-Yong Lie and David Esre (eds.), *Professional Social Service Delivery in a Multicultural World*. Toronto: Canadian Scholars' Press.

_____. 2000a. "North-South Collaborations: Effecting Transnational Perspectives for Social Work." *Journal of Progressive Human Services* 11, 1.

_____. 2000b. "Students at risk in the practicum." In L. Cooper and L. Briggs (eds.), *Human Services Practicum*. New South Wales: Allyn and Unwin.

_____. 2000c. "Shifting positions: Making meanings in social work." In L. Napier and J. Fook (eds.), *Breakthroughs in Practice: Theorising Critical Moments in Social Work*. London: Whiting and Birch.

_____. 2001. "Diversity and difference in the field education encounter: Racial minority students in the practicum." *Social Work Education* 19, 4.

Razack, N., and D. Jeffery. 2001. "Critical race discourse and tenets for social work." *Canadian Social Work Review*. Under review. 2002-Resubmitted.

Razack, N., E. Teram, and M. Rivera. 1995. "Cultural diversity in field work education: A practice model for enhancing cross-cultural knowledge." In G. Rogers (ed.), *Social Work Field Education: Views and Visions.* Dubuque, IA: Kendall/Hunt.

Razack, S. 1998. *Looking White People in the Eye: Gender, Race, and Culture in Courtrooms and Classrooms.* Toronto: University of Toronto.

Reeser, L., and R. Wertkin. 1997. "Sharing sensitive student information with field instructors: Responses of students, liaisons, and field instructors." *Journal of Social Work Education* 33, 2.

"Research Bulletin." 1996. Toronto, ON: Metro Days of Action Research Department.

Roche, S., M. Dewees, R. Trailweaver, S. Alexander, C. Cuddy and M. Handy. 1999. *Contesting Boundaries in Social Work Education.* Alexandria, VA: Council on Social Work Education.

Rodwell, M., and A. Blankebaker. 1992. "Strategies for Developing Cross-Cultural Sensitivity: Wounding as Metaphor." *Journal of Social Work Education* 28, 2 (Spring/Summer).

Roediger, D. 1994. *Towards the Abolition of Whiteness.* London: Verso.

Rogers, G. 1992. "Teaching and learning ethnically-sensitive, antidiscriminatory practice: Field placement principles for Canadian social work programmes." A paper presented at CASSW Annual Conference, Charlottetown, P.E.I.

_____. (ed.). 1995. *Social Work Field Education: Views and Visions.* Dubuque, IA: Kendall/Hunt.

_____. 1996. "Training field instructors British style." *Journal of Social Work Education* 32, 2 (Spring/Summer).

Rompf, E.L., D. Royse, and S.S. Dhooper. 1993. "Anxiety preceding field work: What students worry about." *Journal of Teaching in Social Work* 7, 2.

Rosenblum, A., and F. Raphael. 1983. "The role and function of the faculty field liaison." *Journal of Education of Social Work* 19, 1.

_____. 1987. "Students at risk in the field practicum and indications for field teachers." *The Clinical Supervisor* 5, 3.

Rossiter, A. 1995. "Entering the Intersection of Identity, Form, and Knowledge: Reflections on Curriculum Transformation." *Canadian Journal of Community Mental Health* 14, 1 (Spring).

_____. 1996. "Perspective on critical social work." *Journal of Progressive Human Services* 7, 2.

_____. 2000. "The professional is political: An interpretation of the problem of the past in solution-focused therapy." *American Journal of Orthopsychiatry* 150–61.

_____. 2001. "Innocence lost and suspicion found: Do we educate for or against social work?" *Critical Social Work*, 2, 1.

Rossiter, A., I. Prilletinsky and R. Walsh Bowers. 1996. "Learning from Broken Rules: Individualism, Organization and Ethics." *Proceedings,* Joint Work Congress of the International Federation of Social Workers and the International Association of Schools of Social Work, Hong Kong, July.

Royse, D., S. Dhooper and E. Rompf. 1999. *Field Instruction: A Guide for Social Work Students*. Third edition. New York: Longman.

Salcido, R.M., and J.A. Garcia. 1997. "A comparative analysis of three cross-cultural training approaches: In search of cross-cultural competence." *Arete* 22, 1 (Spring/Summer).

Salcido, R.M., J. Garcia, V. Cota, and C. Thomson. 1995. "A cross-cultural training model for field education." *Arete* 20, 1.

Sanders, D. 1977. "Developing a Graduate Social Work Curriculum with an International Cross-Cultural Perspective." *Journal of Education for Social Work* 13, 3.

Schneck, D. 1991. "Ideal and Reality in Field Education." In D. Schneck, B. Grossman, and U. Glassman (eds.), *Field Education in Social Work: Contemporary Issues and Trends*. Dubuque, IA: Kendall/Hunt.

_____. 1995. "The Promise of Field Education in Social Work." In G. Rogers (ed.), *Social Work Field Education: Views and Visions*. Dubuque, IA: Kendall/Hunt.

Schneck, D., B. Grossman, and U. Glassman (eds.). 1991. *Field Education in Social Work: Contemporary Issues and Trends*. Dubuque, IA: Kendall/Hunt.

Seebaran, R., and C. McNiven. 1979. "Ethnicity, Multiculturalism and Social Work Education." *Canadian Journal of Social Work Education* 5, 2-3.

Selber, K., M. Mulvaney, and M. Lauderdale. 1998. "A field education model for developing quality agency partnerships. *Journal of Teaching in Social Work* 17, 1-2.

Sheafor, B.W., and L. E. Jenkins. 1982. *Quality Field Instruction in Social Work: Program Development and Maintenance*. New York: Longman.

Sheldon, B. 1978. "Theory and practice in social work: A re-examination of a tenuous relationship. *British Journal of Social Work* 8, 1.

Shulman, L. 1983. *Teaching the Helping Skills: A Field Instructor's Guide*. Alexandria, VA: Council on Social Work Education.

Singleton, S. 1994. "Faculty personal comfort and the teaching of content on racial oppression." *Journal of Multicultural Social Work* 3, 1.

Sink, D.W. 1992. "Response to Federal Cutbacks by Nonprofit Agencies and Local Funding Sources." *New England Journal of Human Services* 11, 3.

Smart, R., and M.M. Gray. 2000. "Working with cultural difference." In L. Cooper and L. Briggs (eds.), *Fieldwork in the Human Services*. St. Leonards, Australia: Allen and Unwin.

Social Planning Council, Metro Community Services, City of Toronto, Planning and Development. 1996. "1995 Community Agency Survey Metropolitan Toronto." Toronto, May.

Spivak, G.C. 1993. *Outside in the Teaching Machine*. New York: Routledge.

Summers, H., and M. Yellow Bird. 1995. "Building relationships with First Nations Communities and Agencies: Implications for field education and practice." In G. Rogers (ed.), *Social Work Field Education: Views and Visions*. Dubuque, IA: Kendall/Hunt.

Syson, L., and M. Baginsky. 1981. *Learning to Practice: A Study of Practice Placements in Courses Leading to the Certificate Qualification of Social Work*. London: Central Council for Education and Training in Social Work.

Taylor, I. 1996. "Reflective learning, social work education and practice in the 21st century." In N. Gould and I. Taylor (eds.), *Reflective Learning for Social Work*. Aldershot: Arena.

Taylor, Z. 1999. "Values, theories and methods in social work education." *International Social Work* 42, 3.

Thompson, N. 1993. *Antidiscriminatory Practice*. London: MacMillan.

Toronto Star. 2000. "Toronto Split on Racial Lines: Study." Friday, July 7.

Towle, C. 1963. *The Learner in Education for the Professions*. University of Chicago Press.

Tracking Impacts Coalition, Metro Toronto. 1996. "Tracking Impacts: Who's tracking What (and How to get it!)." October.

Tsang, N.M. 1998. "Beyond theory and practice integration in social work: Lessons from the West." *International Social Work* 41, 2.

Tully, C., and R. Greene. 1993. "Cultural diversity comes of age: A study of coverage 1970–1991." *Arete* 18, (Summer).

United Way of Greater Toronto. 1999. *Toronto at the Turning Point: Demographic, Economic and Social Trends in Toronto*. Toronto: Allocations and Community Services Department. November.

van Dijk, T. 1987. *Communicating Racism: Ethnic Prejudice in Thought and Talk*. Thousand Oaks, CA: Sage Publications.

Van Soest, D. 1994a. "Impact of social work education on student attitudes and behaviour concerning oppression." *Journal of Social Work Education* 32, 2 (Spring/Summer).

_____. 1994b. "Social work education for multicultural practice and social justice advocacy: A field study of how students experience the learning process." *Journal of Multicultural Social Work* 3, 1.

Van Soest, D., and J. Kruzick. 1994. "The influence of learning styles on student and field instructor perceptions of field placement success." *Journal of Teaching in Social Work* 9, 1/2.

Vayda, E., and M. Bogo. 1991. "A teaching model to unite classroom and field." *Journal of Social Work Education* 27, 3.

Walden, T., and L.N. Brown. 1985. "The integration seminar: A vehicle for joining theory and practice. *Journal of Social Work Education* 21, 1.

Weeks, W. 1981. *Innovative Community Settings: A Guide to Social Work Field Instruction*. School of Social Work, McMaster University.

Whitmore, E., and M. Wilson. 1997. "Accompanying the process: Social work and international development practice." *International Social Work* 40, 1.

Wiebe, M. 1996. "The economy of student practicum labor." *Social Worker* 64, 3, (Fall).

Williams, C. 1999. "Connecting antiracist and anti-oppressive theory and practice: Retrenchment or reappraisal?" *British Journal of Social Work* 29, 2.

Williams, P. 1991. *The Alchemy of Race and Rights: Diary of a Law Professor.* Cambridge: Harvard University Press.

Wilson, J. 2000. "Approaches to supervision in fieldwork." In L. Cooper and L. Briggs (eds.), *Fieldwork in the Human Services.* St. Leonards, Australia: Allen and Unwin.

Wilson, R.J., J. Birkenmaier, R. Banks and M Berg-Weger. 2001. "The integrative seminars: A social work odyssey through curriculum." Paper presented at the Annual Program Meeting of the Council on Social Work Education, Dallas, Texas, March.

Wilson, Tikka Jan. 1997. "Feminism and institutionalized racism: Inclusion and exclusion at an Australian feminist refuge." *Feminist Review* 51 (Spring).

Witkin, S. 1998. "Mirror, mirror on the wall: Creative tensions, the academy, and the field." *Social Work* 43, 5.

Yelaja, S. (ed.). 1988. "Proceedings of the Settlement and Integration of New Immigrants to Canada Conference." Waterloo, Ontario: Wilfrid Laurier University, Centre for Social Welfare Studies.

Yeung, V., and L. Tsor-Kui. 1996. "Factors associated with student satisfaction in social work field placement in Hong Kong." *Proceedings,* Joint Work Congress of the International Federation of Social Workers and the International Association of Schools of Social Work, Hong Kong, July, Vol.11.

York Agency Crisis Cutback Committee. 1996. *City of York: Report on Community Well-Being.* Toronto, September.

Young, I. 1990. *Justice and the Politics of Difference.* Princeton, NJ: Princeton University Press.